HIDDEN CHILD OF THE HOLOCAUST

A *True Story*

Stacy Cretzmeyer

SCHOLASTIC INC.

New York Toronto London Auckland Sydney
Mexico City New Delhi Hong Kong Buenos Aires

This book is dedicated to my loving
parents, whose courage, fortitude,
and foresight saw us through those
dark years between 1939 and 1945.

Also to my husband, Harry, who gave
me the courage and love to find my
lost childhood.

And to my children, Diane and Eric,
and their children, Jordan, Sarai, Jessica,
and Samantha, so that they all may know.

Ruth Kapp Hartz

ISBN 0-439-65346-0

12 11 10 9 8 7 6 5 4 3 2 1   4 5 6 7 8 9/0

Printed in the U.S.A.   40

First Scholastic printing, March 2004

Adapted from YOUR NAME IS RENÉE: Ruth Kapp Hartz's Story As a Hidden Child
in Nazi-Occupied France by Stacy Cretzmeyer.

Used by permission of Oxford University Press, Inc., 198 Madison Avenue, New York, NY 10016.

Excerpt from *The Little Prince* by Antoine de Saint-Exupéry, copyright © 1943 and renewed in
1971 by Harcourt Brace & Company, reprinted by permission of the publisher.

Permission granted to use excerpt from the *Passover Haggadah* from the Prayer Book Press, New York.

Permission granted to use excerpt from *Gates of Prayer: The New Union Prayer Book*,
The Central Conference of American Rabbis, 1975, New York.

Contents

Author's Preface

The circumstances of my collaboration with Ruth Kapp Hartz are themselves a story, one that transformed both our lives. As Ruth and I give more and more presentations to children, young people, and adults about the experience of hidden children in the Nazi era, and about the role of non-Jews who sought to protect Jewish refugees and rescue them from near-certain death, we become increasingly aware that our story is indeed part of the larger story of *Hidden Child of the Holocaust*.

Ruth Hartz was my high school French teacher at Springside School in Philadelphia, Pennsylvania. I knew her then as "Madame Renée Hartz." As a teacher, "Madame" was both challenging and warm, sensitive yet demanding, and she had a quiet dignity and grace about her which to this day commands respect. She was concerned about her students even after they graduated, remained interested in their professional activities, and even now cultivates a lively correspondence with many of them.

By high school, I knew that I wanted to write. I had

developed an interest in the subject of the Holocaust and, specifically, what became of Jewish children in the Holocaust. I knew, by the time I reached college, that I wanted to write about a little-researched, little-documented segment of the Holocaust experience: What became of Jewish children in France during the Nazi occupation? (This was in the early eighties, before the Klaus Barbie trial and other such incidents brought to light more information about the degree to which most of the French population had collaborated with the Nazis.)

In school, as my French teacher, Ruth had never spoken about her experiences as a young Jewish child in Nazi-occupied France. I did not know that she was Jewish, nor that her parents were originally from Germany. At that time, I knew only that she had grown up in Paris, and she had expressed great interest in my writing career. We corresponded, and when I finally decided to go to France to do research for a book about the fate of Jewish children in Nazi-occupied France, I wrote to Ruth and asked her for recommendations of people I might interview and where I might find resources for my research.

Amazingly, Ruth wrote back and confided to me that she, herself, had been a hidden child, and had survived the war due to a network of Resistance fighters who had sheltered her—and her parents—in a village in southern France. Ruth invited me back to Philadelphia to talk about this subject, and as I had plans to return to the area, we met one Sunday morning for brunch.

The first questions Ruth asked me were: "Why do you want to write about this subject? Why is it important to you?" It was my turn to confide in Ruth that, as a fifth-grader, I had heard the personal account of a Catholic woman who had sheltered Jewish families during the early years of the war. She and her husband had smuggled many families to "safe houses," and eventually attracted the attention of Gestapo agents. The woman had been tortured by the Nazis in an effort to force her to disclose the whereabouts of her husband. Her fingernails were torn out, one by one, by her Nazi persecutors, but the woman never confessed. Unfortunately, her husband was eventually captured and murdered by the Nazis. The woman, left a widow, made her way to Paris, where she was taken in by a Catholic religious order. Eventually, she became a nun and lived and worked in the convent. She was transferred to the United States in the sixties and was a staff member at my school in Philadelphia. That was how I came to hear her story.

I never forgot the face or the voice of the woman as she told her story. Perhaps it was the first moment in my life that I thought about the force of evil in the world, and wondered where courage came from. I could not understand how people could allow such evil to take place, yet I was stunned by the woman's heroism in the face of such danger. Why did she and her husband defy Nazi orders, attempting instead to save human lives? So many others, I was told, had not.

I explained to Ruth that I had never forgotten that story, and that I knew I had to write a book about the fate of Jewish children during the Holocaust. As a Catholic, I was particularly interested in what Catholic and other Christian denominations did—or did not do—to help the Jews. I had to know why so few helped and so many turned away. At that stage, I hardly realized the shocking numbers of people who had willingly collaborated with the Nazis during the French occupation. I would soon learn.

Ruth revealed to me that she, herself, had been left at a Catholic convent in southern France, not knowing whether her parents were alive or dead. She began to cry as she told me, "I was left in the street. I was told I was 'an orphan of the war.'" To this day, I believe I was one of the first individuals, outside of her immediate family, with whom Ruth shared this painful aspect of her early childhood. Luckily, Ruth's parents did survive, and she was reunited with them near the end of the war.

Ruth asked me if I would consider writing her story, rather than the book I had planned to write. She said that she wanted to have a written record for her husband and children of her experiences during the war. English was a second language for Ruth, and she expressed great faith in my writing ability. I was incredibly honored that Ruth had asked me to write her story. We talked at great length about our proposed collaboration.

Subsequently, I conducted many interviews with Ruth. I began to piece together the events of this young child's life during the Nazi occupation of France, and I had the privilege of watching the adult Ruth gradually come to terms with the terrifying emotions she had experienced in childhood. In reconstructing the events of her early life story, Ruth slowly began to make peace with her history. She eventually invited me to call her Ruth, no longer Renée.

As Ruth embarked on her personal journey of discovery, I at the same time embarked on a professional journey. As a writer, I was determined to capture the incredible experiences of this young child and her family in the voice of a child. I traveled to France alone and retraced the steps of Ruth and her parents while in hiding. I traveled from Paris to Alençon to Ribérac to St. Juéry, Arthès, and Sorèze. I conducted interviews in France throughout the summer of 1985.

I was able to interview Ruth's parents, as well as relatives of rescuers who had sheltered Ruth and her family. I interviewed French Catholic clergy and religious to whom I had been referred, and asked them why they chose to help the Jewish people, knowing that they risked capture by the Nazis, and possibly death, if they did so. I retrieved Ruth's file at the Oeuvre de Secours aux Enfants (O.S.E.), an organization that, during the war, placed many Jewish children in non-Jewish homes for their protection and ultimately tried to smuggle them to Switzerland and, eventually, to the United States. Ruth had never known about the file, or even about the O.S.E. Through a strange twist of fate, I was directed to the O.S.E.

offices by a man who knew the director of the organization. Without his assistance, I never would have uncovered previously unknown aspects of Ruth's story, and how she came to be placed in a Catholic convent.

All the while, as I conducted my research, I was discovering the voice of the young child, Renée. At that time, the phenomenon of hidden children during the Holocaust was just beginning to be explored. I chose to explore it through the impressions, the emotions, the voice of the young Renée. I knew of no other way to do justice to the story.

Ruth entrusted her experiences to me so that I might tell the story that needed to be told. Although I am the author of the written work, *Hidden Child of the Holocaust*, and Ruth is the subject, we have each been learners during our thirteen-year collaboration. We have been awed by the power of this story to transform its readers, and by the power of our story of friendship and collaboration to convince children and young people that they can make a difference. Children and young people continue to be moved by the idea that a teacher's life could be immortalized by the student with whom she had the courage to share her story. I can honestly say that writing this book was a labor of love and respect for my teacher, whose personal experiences forever changed the way I look at the world.

It has often been said that writers do not actually seek their material, their material finds them. The privilege of writing this manuscript is part of my story as an evolving writer and human being. What greater gift could a teacher give her student?

Stacy Cretzmeyer
July 1, 1998

Ruth Kapp Hartz's Preface

Working on this book with the author, my former student Stacy Cretzmeyer, resulted in more than merely creating an interesting narrative. It also served to document for my family those experiences of my early childhood and, even more importantly, permitted me to face those ghosts and embrace adulthood.

Like many hidden children of the Holocaust, I grew up in total ignorance of the war years. My parents, having suffered so much mental stress as a result of having their families obliterated, did not wish to discuss this painful subject with me. "*C'est trop triste* [It's too sad]," my father responded whenever I would ask any questions. "Let's just look forward and not look back," he would add.

History textbooks in France after the war barely mentioned the Holocaust and the shameful collaboration of the French Vichy government with the Nazis. My thoughts of and relationship to France were simple and untainted. It was only after reading the book *The French Against the French*, by

Milton Dank, a personal friend, that I became aware of the extent of the Vichy collaboration with the Nazis.

As a young adult, I came to the United States, was married, had two children, and became a teacher of French language and literature. My children matured at about the time that the Holocaust deniers began to attract attention. I was extremely upset that these people were receiving any recognition at all, so I resolved that my story, at least, should be added to the documentation of the Holocaust that was being assembled at that time.

Therefore, it was a very happy coincidence that I developed a collaboration with my former student, Stacy Cretzmeyer, who was able to weave my experiences into a compelling narrative of those unhappy times, as seen through the eyes of the child that I was then. It was only because of our special relationship that Stacy was able to draw from me recollections that I had not faced for many years. She was equally adept at interviewing my parents and others who had been part of my life during that difficult period.

I will be forever grateful to her for having helped me find my lost childhood and for presenting my story in such a skillful and sensitive way.

Ruth Kapp Hartz

Acknowledgments

The author gratefully wishes to acknowledge the following persons for their assistance and encouragement during the writing of this book:

Milton Dank; Nora Levin, Professor of History at Gratz College; Joan Adess Grossman; Sister C. Chapuis, Sécrétaire de la Provinciale, Religieuses du Sacré Cœur, who first gave us information regarding Sorèze, and put us in contact with many other sources; Sister Françias DeLinares of Les Religieuses de Notre-Dame de Sion, who shared her recollections with me of Paris during the Occupation years, and her own efforts toward saving Jewish children. Also, we thank Madame Denise Bergon (interviewed by Ruth), who is a Sister of the Order of Notre-Dame de Massip in Capdenac, France. As a religious, she saved over eighty children during the war, and was honored in 1981 for rescuing and hiding Jewish children. I thank, also, Monsieur Sam Taub, who put me in contact with the O.S.E. offices in Paris in July 1985.

We thank, especially, Madame Catherine Schulmann and

Madame Samuel, at O.S.E. in Paris, who spent hours going through files and sharing reflections of the activities of the O.S.E., during the war, with us; Madame Monique Cohen, Archivist of the War Years, at the public library in Toulouse; Father Raymond Vandergrift, Archivist at the Dominican College Library, Catholic University, Washington, D.C.; the Reverend Professor Henry C. Johnson, Jr., Professor of the History of Education and Policy Studies at the Pennsylvania State University and Visiting Professor at Catholic University for two years; Bernard Stehle for his exceptional editorial eye; Madame Josette Marchez, accountant at the present-day school of Sorèze; Monsieur and Madame Alfred Kahn, of Alençon, France, who were kind enough to agree to be interviewed by me; Andrée Fedou, who allowed me to interview her in Arthès; and, above all, to Monsieur and Madame Benno Kapp for their willingness to be interviewed on several occasions, and for sharing many, often painful, memories.

I personally wish to thank the Sisters of the Assumption at the Assumption Convent in Merion, Pennsylvania, for their encouragement, hospitality, and willingness to share insights and reflections with me; Patricia and Philip Turmel, who were enormously helpful in guiding me in the ways of the computer, and who hounded me to complete the manuscript revisions; Trudy McConnell Bazemore at the Georgetown, South Carolina, Public Library for her assistance with my research; and Father John F. Bench for continued encouragement and guidance. Also, to Julie Zimmerman, Biddle Publishing Company, for originally recognizing the merit of the work, and for her careful editing of the manuscript.

I especially wish to thank my parents, Patricia and Charles Cretzmeyer, to whom I will always be deeply indebted. Without their confidence in me, their financial assistance, patience, and support, this book could not have been written.

HIDDEN CHILD OF THE HOLOCAUST

FRANCE, SPRING 1942

PART ONE: ESCAPE

Spring 1942 to August 1942

. . . and He delivered us from the hand of the enemy, and of such as lay in wait by the way.

—Ezra 8:3

"The Marshal Is Coming!"

In the spring, in Toulouse, there were sometimes heavy thunderstorms during the late afternoons. Just before the storms broke, an enormous umbrella of lead-colored clouds lowered over the city, and the street outside our apartment building was momentarily and inexplicably hushed. My Uncle Heinrich's apartment was just around the corner from ours. He lived along the railroad tracks. In the main room of his apartment, there would come a sudden gust of wind, rattling knobs, slamming doors. The curtains would billow at the half-opened windows.

There was a sound like the faint crying of women.

I was always at my uncle's house in the afternoons, after school. That particular spring it rained so often, and I grew so used to the whining of the wind, that I would turn to Uncle Heinrich and say, "There they are again, the whining women."

He would nod from the chair where he was reading. "That's right. Loud and clear today. In a minute, they'll be gone."

The sound frightened me. It was so urgent, so tinged with

sadness. Years later, I sometimes heard it in my sleep.
   "Who are they, Uncle?"
   "The ones we left behind."
   So many times that conversation was replayed in my dreams! It seems that the wind whining through window frames has always reminded me of the sound of women crying, but it was Uncle Heinrich who first put the idea in my head, in Toulouse when I was four.

   It's the end of the day.
   I'm standing in the courtyard outside my school, waiting for my cousin, Jeannette. Minutes pass, and she does not come. Someone from my kindergarten class comes to tell me that Jeannette must have gone home sick, just after noon. I turn and run down the steps and along the courtyard, then into the cobblestone streets of Toulouse.
   I can hear all the noises of the street; it's as if everything comes alive when I am let out of school. The man at the furniture stall shouts to a friend across the street; a woman laughs at something she has overheard. I run past them. I could be anyone. I run past them all, and they do not try to stop me. They do not know that I am Jewish.
   I am bursting with news to tell my uncle, but I am mad at Jeannette for making me wait so long at school. She has probably already told the news to Uncle Heinrich. Jeannette is sixteen, and smart. She knows things, like the history of France. She knows that Toulouse is the capital of southern France. Sometimes, she tries to explain the war to me.
   I have walked these streets with Jeannette so many times that I can find my way by myself with no trouble. I am laughing as I run. This is the first time I've ever gone home from school without Jeannette. Rue de l'Aqueduc, that's the name of my street. I say it to myself over and over, so I won't forget. I turn a corner and pass many shops. Sometimes, I like to walk into the shops, especially when there is candy inside. I like to smell the

chocolate, but I haven't seen any chocolate in a long time. The shops in Toulouse seem half empty. Maman says you can't get things in the stores now that you used to find cheaply before the war. She goes out for food every morning before I am awake.

I pass the signs for the bakery and the bookstore on the corner, *boulangerie* and *librairie*. I peer into the window of the bookstore, because there is a copy of a book about our Marshal, Marshal Pétain, in the window. Just as I reach the streetlight at the corner, a woman comes out of a doorway and blocks my way. I recognize her, but I can't remember her name. Her face scares me.

"Well now, I've been waiting for you, little Renée," she says. "Where are you going in such a hurry?"

How does she know me? "Home," I tell her.

She calls me by the French name that Jeannette gave me when she first took me to school in Toulouse. At home, I am still called Ruth; but in public, everyone must think I am French, and so it was Jeannette, always so wise and practical, who had given me my new name.

"Where do you live?" the lady asks.

I look down at her black shoes and shake my head. "I forget the name of the street," I tell her. I am forbidden to tell anyone where we live, even my friends at school. Maman says it is too dangerous to tell anyone. The woman is staring at me. She is an old lady with gray hair and a fat stomach. Her coat has dust along the hem. It might be chalk dust from school. I think she looks like one of the characters in the story we are reading in my class. She has the face of a mean woman, someone you can't trust.

"How can you be on your way home if you don't know what street you live on?" she asks. Her face is lined. There's a deep furrow between her brows. "Where is Jeannette today?"

I'm confused. I shake my head. Suddenly, I remember where I have seen the lady before. She works at school, in the office. I make up a lie. "I have to go to my friend's house, Monique. She lives up there." I point far up the street, to where it narrows around a bend. "Papa comes to pick me up when his shift is over." My voice is shaky. I swallow several times. Maybe I shouldn't have mentioned Papa. Now she knows he does shift work somewhere in the city.

The woman looks up the street in the direction I am pointing. Then she tries to take my arm, as if she is about to lead me somewhere. Just as her hand touches the sleeve of my sweater, I dart around the corner. I run into a café and hide just inside the door for a long time, until the man behind the counter asks, "Well, what do you want, little girl?" I would like something sweet to drink, but I have no money. I go back outside slowly, walking like a lady. I walk the way we've been taught to walk in school. I will take the long way to our apartment. No one must see me.

I follow the street that goes by the church. I go into the dark church where Jeannette and I have hidden before. When you go into a church, they do not think you are Jewish. It's cool in there, and I hear the whispering of a woman kneeling on one of the straw-bottomed chairs, praying. In her hand, there is a chain of beads. She passes the beads through her fingers, one by one. I watch her as she lights a candle in front of a marble figure.

Sometimes, when there are many people in the church, Jeannette and I sit in the back and imitate them. It is something to do, at least until it is safe to return to the street. We start to giggle, but then we're silent, like the others. We forget what brought us into the church in the first place.

I feel lost in the church without Jeannette. It's so dark, and such a scary place, that I find myself backing away toward the broad wooden door. When I walk back into the street, it's so bright I have to close my eyes. Opening them slowly, squinting, I see that no one is there.

It's safe to go on. At last, I'm almost home. Instead of following the Rue de l'Aqueduc, I turn the corner and walk along the Rue St. Jeanne. Before I go home, I have to tell my news to Uncle Heinrich. Uncle Heinrich is my father's older brother. I run up the two flights of steps to his apartment. Jeannette opens the door to stop my loud banging, and I burst into the room, laughing and out of breath.

It's the scent of his pipe that I am first aware of whenever I go to visit my uncle. I love it. The smoke makes me think of a pine forest; I don't know why. Uncle Heinrich brought the tobacco back from Morocco, where he was sent with the Foreign Legion. Aunt Sophie says he will be very sorry he has smoked his pipe every afternoon because the tobacco pouch is almost empty, and it's difficult to find tobacco in France these days.

"Uncle Heinrich! Guess what! Guess what!"

He looks up from his notebook, and I run over to his desk to greet him. "Pétain is coming to Toulouse! *Le Maréchal* is coming here, to Toulouse!"

He is a bit surprised. He raises his eyebrows as he always does when he thinks I am making up a story.

"And who is this Pétain?" he wants to know. He is testing me to see how much I know about what has been happening in France.

"He is our Marshal!" I prance around the room until Jeannette slams a bowl down on the table.

"Humph!" she says. "Who would want to see him?"

I stare at her. How can she say this about our Marshal? Now I notice that she does not look sick at all. Maybe she came home early to help her boyfriend print pamphlets. She does this sometimes, but it's a secret. Jeannette's boyfriend and several others from the neighborhood are planning to pass out the pamphlets around the apartment building and in the neighborhood. I am not to tell Aunt Sophie, who would be very angry. Jeannette says Pétain is a bad man, that he can't be trusted. He is at Vichy now, making laws against the Jewish people. Jeannette explains that Vichy is the southern town where Pétain is camped, and from which he and his aides govern the unoccupied zone of France. In the pamphlets, there will be articles about the latest laws from Vichy, explaining how they will affect the Jews. "He wants to force us to leave France!" Jeanette says.

"Why?" I ask. "He doesn't know us."

"Now, Jeannette," my uncle steps in. "Ruth doesn't have any idea what you're talking about. Don't fill her head with all of this. We don't know that Pétain is responsible for all our troubles. We'll have to wait and see. He could be playing along with the Germans for the time being, until he thinks the time is right to take matters into his own hands. You've been listening to your friends too much. Much of what they tell you could be alarmist talk."

"I hope, for our sake, that you're right, Papa," Jeannette says quietly. "But it's hard to forget the *Statut des Juifs* of two years ago, which he signed. Don't you realize that because of that statute, we could be interned and sent to live in one of those camps, all because we're considered 'Jewish foreigners?' How would you like to live under police surveillance in some village in the middle of nowhere? You can't convince me that Pétain wasn't behind the statutes." Jeannette turns away and stirs something in a bowl. When her face is serious, she hardly looks like herself. I am used to the Jeannette who smiles all the time, but there are moments like this when she scares me. "I prefer to listen to my friends than to have no idea what is actually going on," she says.

Uncle Heinrich pulls me onto his lap. "Let Ruth go and have her fun," he tells Jeannette. "Let her go and see her Marshal."

I nod. I am determined to go. I will ask Papa to take me, if Jeannette will not. Everyone else from school is going to see the parade. Jeannette will be left behind at her desk with no one to talk to.

"And what else happened today at school?" Uncle Heinrich asks me.

I look up into his kind, dark eyes. I am afraid to tell him, but I've never been able to keep anything from him. "A lady stopped me on the street after school," I tell him. "She was waiting for me. She asked me where I live!"

Jeannette turns sharply around. She and Uncle Heinrich exchange a look I don't understand. "What did she look like?" asks Jeannette.

"She had gray hair. I think she's the old lady who works in the office at school."

"Did she ask you other questions?" Uncle Heinrich wants to know.

"She asked me where Jeannette was and where I was going."

"Did you tell her?"

"No. I said I had to go to my friend Monique's house because Papa was going to pick me up there. Then I ran away."

"Ruth," says Jeannette, very seriously, "did she see where you went? Did she follow you?"

I slip down from Uncle Heinrich's lap and walk over to the window. I look down, over the ledge. There is just the street, a bicycle, a boy. "No. She is not there. Besides, I ran away fast. She couldn't follow me. I hid in the church."

Jeannette and Uncle Heinrich exchange a glance, a look of relief, but they don't say anything. Then Jeannette walks away with the bowl. I follow her into the alcove, where there is a basin.

"You told me to lie if anyone ever asked me where I live, Jeannette. Are we going to get into trouble?"

"I don't think so, Ruth. It was good that you remembered to lie. You did the right thing. But maybe we won't go back to school for a while."

"But I have to. I have to see Marshal Pétain!"

Jeannette doesn't say anything more. Uncle Heinrich calls me over and takes me onto his lap again.

"What are you doing, Uncle?" I ask him in French. *"Qu'est-ce que vous faites, mon oncle?"*

I like this new French sentence I learned at school. I go about asking everyone what they are doing. But at home, I am never sure whether or not my family understands me when I speak in French. My uncle still speaks German most of the time. Sometimes he answers me very slowly, in French. I laugh at his mistakes.

He tells me that he is writing letters to his family in Germany. My two aunts on Papa's side, Sittie and Hettie; my grandmother, Papa's mother; and my great-aunt are all still in Germany as far as we know. Maman's father and stepmother and their daughter, Lottie, may still be there, too. Papa's family lives in a small town called Hechstheim, in the Rhineland. Jeannette showed me the place on the map in school one day after everyone had gone home. She was born in Germany, but I was born in Palestine. Papa has not heard from his family since 1936, when he and Maman left Germany to go to Palestine.

"But Uncle Heinrich, why don't you write to them on a piece of paper and then mail your letter to them?"

"I tried that at first, but my letters were never answered. The letters probably never reached them. It is far better I write to them in the book, and then, after the war is over, our family will be able to read the whole thing at once and will know everything that has happened to us since we left Germany."

"Do you think they are writing to us?"

"I don't know, Ruth. Perhaps."

He turns back some pages in the book and reads to me from a letter dated September 1939. Uncle Heinrich says he wrote the letter in a place called Strasbourg, where he and Aunt Sophie were living. When he reads, his voice is soft, sad. He talks slowly, and you can see the lines in his face clearly because of the afternoon light. It is as if reading the letter somehow makes him older.

Dear Mother:

We were ordered to leave Strasbourg last night. We have time to pack only a few possessions and clothes. The penalty for those who do not leave now will be severe, I'm afraid.

Everyone is heading for the south of France. We

have been assured that we will be safe there. I hope to be gone by dawn, so do not try to write to us here anymore. We will write to you from the South.

I have heard no news from Benno and Lissy. They must get out of Paris soon, or I'm afraid they'll be trapped there—the worst possible thing that could happen to them at this point. We miss you, and hope to hear word from you soon.

"What about me, Uncle Heinrich?" I interrupt. "What happened to me when Maman and Papa had to leave Paris?"

"You were with them, silly. Only you were too much of a baby to know what was happening to you." Jeannette has slipped into a chair, and we listen to my uncle as he reads another letter.

"This was written last year," he tells us. "April 1941, just after I returned from the Foreign Legion. You see, even though we are not French nationals, your Uncle Benno and I were told that by enlisting in the French Foreign Legion, we would escape internment in some camp, and our families would be protected as well." Uncle Heinrich is explaining this very seriously to Jeannette as though for the first time. I don't understand everything he is saying. "There were so many of us who joined the Legion, mostly to protect our families; and there we were, with the French forces in May of 1940, but some later became prisoners and were interned in forced labor camps."

Dear Family:

I have returned from Morocco, and we are now all together in Toulouse. I do not recognize Jeannette. She has grown up in the long months since I've been gone.

Benno returned from the Foreign Legion several days ago. He got to Marrakech and Fez. We will have many stories to tell you when this war is over. Both of us made many friends in the Legion; they become your second family, since your own is so far away. Looking back, I realize how smart we were to join the Legion. By joining, we saved our families from being taken to the concentration camps. We hear now that all the refugees who do not hold French citizenship are sent to the French camps called Gurs, Rivesaltes, Les Milles. Benno and I escaped this, only because we joined the Legion. Even so, some of our friends have been detained as prisoners, and we have not heard from them.

We will be safe here, for the time being. We are in the free zone, the section of France which is not occupied by the Nazis. Everyone wonders how long the situation will last, but how fortunate we all are to have made it this far! Nowadays, many do not make it across the demarcation line which divides the Nazi-occupied north from Vichy France. Without a guide, a non-Jew to help one across the line, it is almost hopeless. One often sees children, traveling alone, on foot. You can only guess at what they have escaped.

Benno and I wish you could be here with us. We are always thinking of you. Sophie and Jeannette send their love.

It's strange to hear my uncle read to me about my own parents, using their names. It's as if they're in a story, and their lives are separate from my own. I remember Papa coming home from the Legion, but I don't remember how he saved us from going to a concentration camp. I don't know what it means.

My uncle turns a page and is about to read another letter when Jeannette jumps up from her chair.

She says, "Let's play a game, Renée!"

To Jeannette, I am like a little doll. She plays games with me, looks after me whenever Maman goes out. My favorite entertainment is to brush her hair while she tells me stories about what our lives are going to be like when we are grown.

She is my big sister who takes me everywhere. Some say we even look like sisters, because we both have slanting eyes. If I were sixteen, I could do all the things she does.

Uncle Heinrich says, "Renée will have to be getting home soon."

"He's right," says Aunt Sophie, coming out of the small bedroom, just off the alcove. "It's after five o'clock. Lissy will be worried. You walk her home, Jeannette."

In the afternoons, Aunt Sophie takes a nap. You can tell she has been sleeping. There is a crease on her cheek from resting her head on the coverlet. She is putting on her apron, and she stops a minute before the mirror to brush her short hair. Her curving eyebrows make her look wide awake. Maman says Aunt Sophie did not come from Germany, but from another country, called Poland. That's why she speaks in a strange accent. She loves Uncle Heinrich very much; ever since he has come back, they are always together. Uncle Heinrich closes his book and kisses my cheek. I put on my sweater, and Jeannette buttons it for me. I want to stay. I want to have dinner and listen to Uncle Heinrich's stories, but I turn and kiss my aunt good night. Then Jeannette and I are on our way down the stairs, and out into the warm spring evening. Jeannette stops at the doorway to put up her long, dark hair. Then she turns to me, smiles with her dark eyes, and takes my hand.

I ask her what the place was like where my parents lived before, called Paris.

"Oh, it's hard to remember," she says, looking down. We follow the sidewalk, turning onto the Rue de l'Aqueduc. "It's a big city. I have only been there once, with Papa. It's filled with old, beautiful buildings and museums. People call it the capital of the civilized world and say that all the other cities can't compare to it."

"Did Maman and Papa live in a beautiful house?"

Jeannette laughs. "No, Renée. Your parents had to live in a small room while they were there. At one time, it must have been somebody's bedroom. There wasn't much furniture. A table and two chairs, a bed. I think you spent a lot of time with your Uncle Oscar's family."

Uncle Oscar is Maman's only brother. I think I remember him, but Maman says I am too young to remember the last time we saw him. I am sad, somehow, thinking that my parents did not live in a beautiful house.

"Why did we have to leave Paris?"

Jeannette's face grows serious. "Because, Renée, there were people there who wanted to round up you and your family, and everyone who was not born in France, and send them all out of the country."

"But why would they want to do that?"

Her hand tightens around mine. "They think the people who were born in other countries don't belong here. Even though we have come to France and our parents have worked hard to keep their homes, these people want to take them from us. It's because we're Jewish." She stops in the middle of the pavement and looks all around. She wants to make sure that no one heard what she just said. I look up at her deep brown eyes, her dark hair, her kind face, and I don't believe anyone will try to harm us. I know Jeannette will protect me as long as I stay with her.

She bends down and looks into my face. "Renée," she whispers, "you must pretend that you didn't hear what I just said. Never, ever, say that word. Even if someone questions you, pretend you don't know what it means."

"But why, Jeannette?"

"It's a long story," she says, taking my hand again. "You'll understand someday. I think that's the reason why that woman waited for you after school today. Be careful of people like her. Don't trust anyone outside of our family."

We've come to the apartment building where I live. Many of the flowers out front have begun to bloom. Jonquils and daffodils line the walk. They make me think that this is a nice place to live, but Maman is not happy in the apartment. She hates the peeling paint on the walls inside our room, the smell, the stairway that shakes when you walk up or down the steps. I notice Maman has been waiting for me just inside the door.

"Where have you been, *mon petit chou?*" she scolds me, but still calling me her little cabbage, in French. "Thank you, Jeannette, for bringing her home."

"Maman, Maman! Guess what!"

"What?" She and Jeannette are laughing, looking down at me. "What is it?"

And I tell my news all over again. "*Le Maréchal! Le Maréchal* is coming to Toulouse! Everyone in school is allowed to go to the parade and see him. Can we go, Maman?"

Maman does not answer. I run up the stairs to look for our friend, Sylvie, who lives on *le premier étage*, the first floor above the ground floor. I want everyone in the building to know that Pétain is coming. But Sylvie does not answer her door.

Maman and Jeannette are talking in low tones at the bottom of the stairs. I listen to Jeannette telling Maman about the woman who waited for me in the street, after school. Maman's face looks serious, anxious. She shakes her head and says, "*Oh, non, non,*" in her low voice. Jeannette gives Maman advice. She knows what is going on in the neighborhood; it's Maman who is too afraid to go out, unless she has to. So she listens to Jeannette, whom she calls her "little spy."

Soon, Jeannette is gone, and Maman calls for me to go downstairs. She does not look at me, and she is frowning. I know what it means. I will not be allowed to go to school tomorrow. I might not be allowed to see Marshal Pétain.

Most afternoons, my uncle read to me from his book of letters; but sometimes, it was Le Petit Chaperon Rouge [Little Red Riding Hood] *or some other Mother Goose story in French. Often, I would see him jotting down notes on a piece of paper, little things he wanted to remember to write to his sisters. He was a learned man, more intellectual, perhaps, than my own father, and he was determined to* record all that had happened to our family in his book.

There was an old armoire to the right of the window in his apartment, left vacant and somewhat ajar by the previous tenants, who had deserted the room in haste several days before my uncle and his family got there. Uncle Heinrich kept his book in one of the drawers. The stories in the book were about places and events I could not remember; yet, my name appeared often enough for me to be curious about what happened to me next. I begged Uncle Heinrich to read all the parts about me. I wondered about that gray period of time during which I had been "preconscious." So many important events had occurred, events which brought me to the place where I was now, but I had no recollection nor understanding of these events. Much of what Uncle Heinrich read to me made no sense: What were concentration camps? What was the demarcation line? What was Paris like? Yet he read the letters over and over until the stories became memories in my mind, and I could not forget them.

I never knew my grandmother and my two aunts. I believed I knew their voices, but that was the closest I could come to them. Uncle Heinrich told me that if I listened to the wind for a long time, I would hear Sittie and Hettie crying. He never told me why he thought they were crying. I was to find that out for myself.

I kept remembering strange, half-lit rooms. These rooms in my memory were the various places we had lived until our arrival in Toulouse. I would describe a piece of furniture to Maman, or a certain pattern of upholstery, and she would say, "That was in the apartment in Alençon"; or, "Aunt Hanna bought that before she left for St. Juéry." The names meant nothing to me, and because I could hardly recall being in those places, Toulouse was my first "home." I went to the school there and spoke the language. I had been exposed to enough French that I could never have been mistaken for a refugee. I had thought of myself as French from my earliest memories. That spring of 1942, I was not quite five years old.

Waiting for Papa

Maman and I had arrived in Toulouse nearly two years before, in the summer of 1940, after months of traveling and hiding. Papa had been away, in the French Foreign Legion, for almost a year and a half when Maman and I finally arrived in the southern two-fifths of France known as *la zone libre*, the free zone.

We had come by train, with Hanna, Raymonde, and Evelyne, wife and children of my mother's brother, Oscar. After our departure from the Dordogne region, where we had fled soon after the Nazis had occupied Paris, we drove for hours just to reach a railroad station that was on the same line as Toulouse. Hundreds of Jewish families were making their way south, to the unoccupied zone, in a similar manner. As refugees, we traveled at great risk: the Vichy government's plan was to expel all foreign Jews from the unoccupied zone in France before they could further upset the ailing French economy, appropriating jobs and businesses that the government claimed should be controlled and operated only by French citizens.

Thus, the Vichy authorities attempted to redirect the refugees into the occupied zone, where they would be at the mercy of the German occupying forces. But the Germans would have none of it; the occupied zone, like all of Germany, and eventually all of Europe, was supposed to be *Judenrein,* or "purified of Jews."

In August of 1940, the demarcation line was abruptly closed on both sides so that the Jews could only travel to the unoccupied zone illegally. Had Maman and I been caught on our way to Toulouse in 1940, we probably would have been thrust back into the occupied zone and eventually deported. Several times, Maman thought we would be singled out and turned in, but we kept moving often enough that we were never caught. And so we finally did reach the South.

Maman knew that Uncle Heinrich and his family had come from Alsace to Toulouse, a large city where they would have a better chance of being absorbed. She knew that my uncle would help us find a place where we could live until Papa returned from the war, but when we arrived in Toulouse, Maman discovered that Uncle Heinrich, too, had joined the Foreign Legion and would be gone indefinitely.

Maman was eventually able to establish for us a kind of home in Toulouse; our main preoccupations, then, became waiting for Papa to return to us and finding enough food to survive. Our room, which was without electricity, had the minimum necessities: a kerosene lamp, a bed for Maman, and a small day-bed for me. We felt our building shake whenever a trolley car went by. Later, when Uncle Heinrich returned from the Legion, he found a table and two chairs and gave them to Maman for our apartment.

Maman had to leave the apartment very early in the mornings to stand in line at the market in the large square that encompassed Le Capitole, a grand building that dominated the center of the square. She would dress while it was still dark and would be gone before daybreak. I would wake to the sound of her shoes clomping down the front steps, and then along the cobblestone street beyond the window. There might be a piece of candy by my bed. This meant that Maman was standing in line at the market, waiting for food, and would be home soon. Maman always did her errands early in the morning, believing that this was the only time that food was available. This habit also lessened her chances of being observed. In a city, your fate could go either way, but you had to eat. Many mornings she came home with an embarrassed look on her face because she had not realized, until she got outside and could see, that she was wearing one blue stocking and one brown.

I remember that the stores had very little to sell. Aunt Sophie and Jeannette took turns going out to the farmers in the neighboring villages to get food. In big cities, such as Toulouse, you could get certain foods through the "black market," but the prices were terribly high. Maman tried to sell some of the linens that she had been able to bring with her into hiding, but only when she was desperate.

Everything was rationed, including our clothing. In the cities, all sorts of foods were impossible to obtain during the winter. There were days when Maman would return from the market empty-handed. For supper on those nights, our meal consisted of a few slices of bread.

"I'm sorry," Maman would apologize, "but it's all I have."

Maman also worried constantly about our relatives who were still in Germany. Rumors and reports of pogroms, arrests, and concentration camps were everywhere. The more she heard, the more she hoped and prayed that our relatives might somehow find a way to follow us into hiding. Once in Toulouse, however, Maman was unable to make any contact with them.

I was four and a half years old, but I could remember Papa, and the apartment seemed empty without him. I was afraid he would not come back at all. Maman told me I must never forget Papa, nor the fact that we still had family in Germany. She taught me that my relatives were a vital part of my life, that they were my family; but it was difficult to remember relatives I had never seen, and neither Maman nor I could have imagined what they were suffering in Germany. I only understood that we were in the middle of a war, and that our lives were in danger because we were not French. We were Jewish.

I asked Maman once why Grand-maman and my two aunts had not come with Papa when he left Germany in 1936.

"Papa begged them to," Maman explained, "but they laughed at him. They thought he was crazy to leave Germany. They did not want to disrupt their lives. Most people thought Hitler would be defeated quickly, and the uproar would soon die down."

However, we felt fortunate to have been reunited with one part of our family. We spent many happy hours with Aunt Sophie and Jeannette.

At the end of that summer, Jeannette took me to the École Maternelle in Toulouse and enrolled me in the kindergarten. When asked to give my name, Jeannette responded emphatically, "Her name is Renée." And that is how I came by my French name. From that day on, I walked to and from school with Jeannette, while some of the local school boys lagged several paces behind, not wanting to be seen walking with the girls. Jeannette taught me never to admit to anyone that I was Jewish, especially in school, and never to use my real name in public. She made sure I remembered these lessons; she devised games in which she would pretend to be different people meeting me for the first time, and she would scold me if ever I let on in any way that I was either German or Jewish.

I did not have a good experience at the school, and was often made fun of by the other children, not because they knew I was Jewish, but simply because I was new. All the kindergarten children were in one room, and, because we were so young, we did little more than play supervised games. I lived for the end of the day when Jeannette would stop by my classroom for me and walk me home. Often she would come over to our one-room apartment and look after me while Maman washed clothes or ran an errand.

Sometimes, when I misbehaved and Jeannette was not available to look after me, Maman would lock me in the coal cellar behind our building. She was always afraid when I acted up. I would draw attention to our room, if not to the entire building. I was often noisy, and a noisy child was most unwelcome in a building where so many stateless Jews were in hiding from the French police and the informers who were everywhere in Toulouse. With the passage of time, we adjusted to our increasingly precarious situation. We relinquished more and more freedom, until we realized, finally, that we had none at all. For Maman, memories were gradually replaced by the cruel realities of life in wartime France, and the threat of the Nazis overtaking the South. She spoke so little of Germany in those days, I began to wonder whether she had actually lived there.

Uncle Heinrich returned from the Legion in October of 1940, well before Papa.

He had been away for a little over a year, but except for a brief time in the beginning of their tours of duty, he had not come in contact with Papa. I was drawn to my uncle from the start, perhaps because I missed having a father so much. I remember how Uncle Heinrich looked in his uniform, which he sometimes put on in the evenings when he was telling his stories about Morocco. Uncle Heinrich was much taller than Papa, and he was tanned and handsome. His features were irregular, but he had the kind, dreamy eyes that Jeannette had inherited. Sophie and Jeannette were so happy to see him that they could not possibly have disguised the relief and love they felt just to have him seated at one end of the dinner table.

Unfortunately, their happiness seemed to increase Maman's suffering. She was so worried about Papa and could not understand why he had not returned on the ship with Heinrich. In those days, Maman was often moody and emotional, and I found it difficult to be at home without Jeannette. I always wanted to play with my cousin or to talk to Uncle Heinrich, but Maman's sadness frightened me, and I sometimes drew away from her.

One morning in 1941 I was looking out our window, and I noticed a man walking up the street. I watched this man for several minutes before I ran out into the hallway and opened the door to the building. For some reason, as I stood there in the doorway, I called, "Papa! Papa!" although I didn't recognize the man at all. He looked up the street, spotted me, and smiled. When he waved back, I knew he must be my father. Maman followed me out into the hall and stood behind me, peering out into the street. The next thing I knew, she was running into the street and calling my father's name. She put her arms around the man in the uniform and began to cry. I had never seen her cry so much. Yes, it was really Papa! I ran over to them, and the man lifted me up into his arms. Now Maman was laughing. The man picked two flowers from the garden in front of our building and gave one to Maman and one to me. Then he carried me into our apartment and held us close for a long time.

Papa sat in a chair while Maman began to prepare our lunch. "You've lost so much weight!" she told Papa. He answered, "You're a fine one to talk!" Maman laughed. She had not laughed like that in a long time. I told Papa about my new school, about my cousin Jeannette, and how I had learned to speak French. Each time he called me Ruth, I corrected him and explained that my name was Renée, that Jeannette had told me very firmly on the way to school that first morning, "Your name is Renée." Papa nodded and exchanged a glance with Maman. "This is a good thing," he said to her.

Maman explained how Jeannette had trained me to behave as a French child. Maman also told Papa about the man who lived next door and worked at the Préfecture (the official residence of the chief magistrate in the area).

"Do you think he can be trusted?" Papa asked.

"Yes," Maman said. "He has been very kind and helpful to us."

Papa was tan, and Maman said that in his uniform, he was more handsome than she remembered. "But I am glad you don't have to wear it anymore," she added.

I remember being afraid to go to sleep that night. I thought that when I woke up, Papa would be gone again. He shook his head and told me he would not go away anymore. In his low, gentle voice, he told me stories about Morocco until I fell asleep.

Papa found a job working in a scrap metal factory in Toulouse, called Tabule. He worked illegally, from eight in the morning until six at night. Maman continued to travel with Aunt Sophie to the neighboring farms for vegetables. Jeannette and I attended school regularly, and, as far as we knew, no one suspected we were Jewish.

Life was almost normal.

Now that Uncle Heinrich and Papa had returned from the Legion, our two families spent much of our time together. For the first time in my life, I felt as if I was living in a family environment. Uncle Heinrich was concerned that I was not making sufficient progress in reading, so I would go to visit him after school, and he would help me practice. I spent hours at his apartment, and a great friendship developed between my uncle and me, much to the concern of Maman, who felt I should be at home, inside with her, at all times.

In school, I learned about Marshal Henri Philippe Pétain, the hero of Verdun. Our teacher told us that the Marshal was a wise and dedicated soldier who was helping to rebuild France, in spite of the chaos of war. She hung his picture on the wall of our classroom, so that we no longer had to imagine what he looked like when she talked about him.

One day that spring, our teacher told us that Pétain himself would soon be coming to Toulouse. There would be a grand parade along the Place Jean Jaurès, and the Marshal was to give a speech to the people of the city. I begged Papa to take me to see the Marshal. My teacher had made it clear that Pétain was bestowing a great honor upon the city in choosing Toulouse to visit, and it was our duty to welcome him. He was particularly interested in addressing the children of France in many of his speeches.

Papa hesitated before saying anything. He tried to explain to me that it would be too dangerous for us to attend a parade. Because we were not truly French, he explained, we did not have to be as patriotic as everyone else. The more I insisted, however, the more Papa wavered. At last, Maman intervened. "It might appear strange to the teacher if she notices that one or two of her students are not present to greet the Marshal," Maman said.

"How will she be able to notice anything in a crowded parade?" Papa wanted to know.

"Perhaps," said Maman gently, "they are all going together, in a group. Do you want Ruth to feel left out?"

"If they're going in a group, that's their choice. I will take Ruth myself."

Maman smiled at me. She was concerned that, in countless ways, we were constantly revealing our background as Jewish-German refugees. She told us many times that we had to learn to act as any other French family would act in Toulouse. If the other students were going to see Pétain, then I, too, must go. Papa agreed that it was, after all, a historic event. But he was right to be anxious. In a matter of months, the French "free zone" would disappear, and we would find ourselves running not only from the French police, but from the German Gestapo as well. Marshal Pétain would soon become a mere figurehead for the French people, many of whom would eventually condemn him as a traitor to France.

Last Train from Toulouse

We're standing on the sidewalk in the middle of a crowd of people on the Place Jean Jaurès, a public square. Maman has not come with us to see the parade. The crowd is noisy; everyone is excited and waiting to see the Marshal. I have never seen so many people before. Everyone is looking in the same direction, but all I can see are the dark skirts and pant legs of the people standing in front of me.

"The cars are coming," Papa tells me.

I pull on his arm until he lifts me onto his shoulders. Now I can see all of it. I see the black, open cars coming along the street. The Marshal is getting nearer, and behind his cars, the parade of Legionnaires of Toulouse-Pyrenées. Papa tells me to wave. All around us, people are waving hats and gloves and flags. The crowd is in a fervor of joy and expectation as the Marshal approaches. I love the noise. People shout "*Vive le Maréchal!*" and some begin to sing "La Marseillaise" and chant "Marshal, we are here!" We have confetti to throw up into the air. It looks like colored snow and lands on the hair of the woman in front of me. Papa says it looks as if all of Toulouse is here in the square, plus he has heard there are over 20,000 Legionnaires. People are shoving their way through the crowd. Some of the people, standing in a small group behind us, are angry and shout things at the oncoming cars. I don't know why. Papa listens to what these people are saying among themselves. Maybe they are Jewish, like us, and frightened.

Papa moves along the sidewalk so I can see the cars coming up the street. He moves behind the column of people. He can't see anything. We find a new place, next to a tree, where we have a better view. Papa says the Marshal is not in the first car, but in the second or third. He will soon get out and wave and talk to the crowd. I can see my teacher from school, but she does not see me. We wait a long time. The cars move slowly along the avenue and pass us by. "I see him! I see him!" I shout, although I am not sure I really have. Papa says the Marshal is the white-haired man standing in the open car, who salutes as he turns to his left and right. All the men in the cars are wearing hats and waving at me.

The cars turn a corner. We do not see them anymore. There is a long wait. I see Monique, my friend from school. She is standing with her parents on the other side of the street. I tell Papa who she is. He just smiles and nods. I am so glad Monique can see my father. For so long, I've had to tell everyone at school that Papa was away in the war. Now, they can all see that I have a father, just like they do.

There is more cheering, and cries of welcome. Everyone applauds. If I get down on the sidewalk and sit on the curb, I can see through everyone's legs, but Papa says I won't see the Marshal that way. A white-haired man climbs up onto the platform in the center of the square. He has a mustache. I know it is the Marshal because of his white hair. "That's him, Papa!" I say, and Papa nods. I wave. I see him very clearly. He holds his hand to his hat. Papa says it is a salute. Marshal Pétain is wearing a dark military coat. Everyone is shouting, "*Vive le*

Maréchal!" but Papa does not shout; he does not say anything.

The Marshal shakes hands with the mayor of Toulouse. Then he presents the national Legion flag. The moment is solemn, and there is a hushed silence. Marshal Pétain holds up his hands and begins to talk. Everyone quiets down to listen. He talks about a union among all Frenchmen. Everyone must help to rebuild France. It is our duty. "All must help to realize this union among people that is so necessary to the salvation of France," he says.

The Marshal talks for only a short time. His voice booms over the street. This is because of the microphone he uses. I do not understand everything that the Marshal says. He is a very old man. It is afternoon, and the sun is warm on my face. The Marshal wipes his forehead with a handkerchief. He stops talking, and the cheering starts again. Papa lowers me to the ground. I cannot see where the Marshal has gone. Papa takes my hand, and we walk away from the crowd. He wants to go home, but I want to stay and wait for the cars. Papa says it is a long way back to our apartment. The wind whips up dust and blows it into my eyes. All the people are pressed against one another and against the metal barricades, waiting for the Marshal to reappear.

"I don't know where all the people come from," Papa says.

We stop in a café and sit by the window. Papa orders a fake coffee and lets me take a sip. He says it is made out of chicory. He doesn't like it, but he drinks it anyway. You can't get real coffee in France anymore, he says. Papa asks me again about the gray-haired lady who stopped me in the street after school a few weeks ago. "What did you say to her?" he asks me again. "Have you seen her since then?" I can't remember. Why is it so important? Papa explains to me that the woman might be an informer, someone who gives away the location of Jews who are in hiding.

"She is a mean lady," I tell Papa.

He looks over my head, out the window, and the dust keeps blowing in the street.

We leave the café and keep walking. It is early summer, and the trees in Toulouse are a deep green, full of leaves. There are flowers in boxes outside the doors of some of the houses. Papa holds my hand, but he does not say anything.

"Do you like Marshal Pétain, Papa?" I ask him.

Papa looks down the street. "Oh, I don't know. What do you think, my little Renée?"

"I like him, Papa. He is my Marshal. But he is very old to be the Marshal of France."

Papa just laughs. I cannot wait to tell Jeannette about the parade.

School is out in Toulouse. It's summer, and Maman says the heat is getting to her. Our apartment is too small, she says. We have only one window.

Papa says, "We're lucky to have what we have."

Maman thinks that maybe it is time for us to look for a new place. Too many people know this building. But I'm used to where we live now, and I'm tired of moving. Maman misses a way of life I've never known.

Jeannette asks me to help her cook. Tonight will be the beginning of the Sabbath, and she has invited someone over for dinner. He is a boy who works at a printing shop several blocks away. I am allowed to help Jeannette get dressed. She has made leek soup for her friend. Because it is a special night, I will have to go home soon. Jeannette says I can see her friend another time. I ask her to tell me about observing the Sabbath, but she says there is not time tonight. My parents have not observed the Sabbath since they came to France, but Uncle Heinrich insists that he will always observe it in his home, no matter what the danger.

"You will spend next Sabbath with us, Renée," Jeannette promises, "if your parents will let you stay that late. Now how do I look?" She turns around and around. She is wearing a skirt that Maman helped her sew. Somewhere,

Jeannette found a necklace of green beads, and she puts it on.

Uncle Heinrich comes into the room. "Beautiful, Jeannette!" he says.

I stand on a chair and comb out Jeannette's long curls. I love to make the curls turn under my fingers.

Soon, there is a knock at the half-open door. It is Papa. He's home from the factory early. He comes into the room. When he sees Jeannette, he raises his eyebrows and whistles. Uncle Heinrich tells Papa to pull up a chair and they will have some wine together. Aunt Sophie is in the next room, getting dressed. She wants to look nice for Jeannette's friend. Papa turns to Uncle Heinrich and nudges his arm. "A beauty," he says. He is talking about Jeannette. Uncle Heinrich nods and smiles. "You'll have one, too, in a couple of years."

I climb off the chair and run to Uncle Heinrich. "Will you read to me, Uncle? Please? Just for a little while, before I have to go?"

He laughs, and I take out my favorite book, *Le Petit Chaperon Rouge*. He starts to read the story to me, but I already know it by heart. I follow the words with my finger. Uncle Heinrich holds my hand over each word as he reads it. Aunt Sophie comes into the room all dressed up. "Ah, another beauty!" Papa says, standing up. Aunt Sophie smiles and turns around in a circle.

"Come, Renée," Papa tells me. He is looking at his watch. "It's seven o'clock. Time to get back. Maman will be worried."

"I want to stay and eat here!"

Jeannette laughs, shaking her head. Aunt Sophie puts her arms around me and says, "You eat with us tomorrow night, Renée. All right?"

"Yes, thank you."

"*Bonsoir!*" Papa calls as he closes the door. I hear Uncle Heinrich and Aunt Sophie calling goodbye. We walk down the steps and into the quiet street. It is still light out. For a moment,

Papa stands there, looking up into the sky. He breathes deeply, and we hear crickets all around, singing. We turn the corner and walk up the front path to our own apartment. Inside, Papa pauses at the window to the right of the front door. We stand there looking at the street. A boy walks by. Papa says it must be Jeannette's friend. He laughs a little. "Looks like a nice boy," he says. Then he turns away from the window. He says he has a strange feeling, but he can't say why.

Maman is waiting with our supper ready. "Where have you been? I was worried!" She always says that. Papa thinks it's good when Maman's worried. When she stops worrying, then he knows something will go wrong.

"I had a glass of wine with Heinrich," Papa says.

We tell Maman all about Jeannette's skirt, and about the boy walking by in the street. Maman thinks it's dangerous for the boy to be out in the streets when it's still light out. He could draw attention to our building. We know that many Jews are under surveillance, or have already been taken away. Papa just shrugs. I walk over to the window and check to see that no one is following Jeannette's friend. There is no one there.

We sit down to eat our supper. As we begin to eat, the floorboards creak out in the hallway; there is a knock on the door. Maman and Papa look at each other across the table. Papa is holding a piece of bread in midair. Maman and Papa keep looking at each other. "What's wrong?" I whisper. Maman slowly stands up as Papa goes to the door. There is more knocking. Papa, in a low voice, says, "*Oui?*"

"It's Lambert," a voice says, on the other side of the door.

Maman sits down, relieved. She tells Papa it is the man who works in the Préfecture. Papa opens the door, and the man bursts into the room. He is out of breath. He has run all the way to our building. He tells Papa to close the door. Maman stands up again. She is holding my hand. The man looks nervous, tired. He is overweight and is still breathing heavily from having run so far.

"You have to get out! Fast! I heard it at work today. They know all about the building. There's going to be a roundup, probably within the hour! You cannot wait another minute."

Papa swallows. Maman is already throwing things into a bag. She takes a little box out from under the mattress and puts it into the bag. I know that it is the box of money. She throws my clothes into the bag then, and her own clothes. Papa is about to go out the door.

"Where are you going, Benno?" Maman asks. Her eyes are wide.

"I have to go over and warn Heinrich."

Monsieur Lambert whispers, "Are you crazy? There's no time. I'll warn him. What floor does he live on?"

Papa's eyes become narrow slits. "How do we know you aren't trying to set us up?" he asks. "We'll get to the train station, and you'll have the police there waiting to arrest us."

"Benno!" Maman cries. "This man has helped us so much. Why would he want to set us up now?"

"You'll just have to believe me, Monsieur," the man says, "unless you want to be arrested here, in the building."

Papa tells the man where to find Uncle Heinrich. The man nods and looks at his watch. "I'll go there right now. You have my word. But get out of here as soon as you can. There's a train leaving for Albi in ten minutes," he tells us. "It's the last train leaving tonight. I'll warn your brother, but you'd better hurry and get out of here."

Then he is gone.

Maman is already finished packing our things. I begin to cry. "What about Jeannette?"

Maman shakes her head. "She will be right behind us, Renée."

We are all whispering, as if the police are already outside. Papa puts his hat on and we go to the door. Maman turns around and looks regretfully at the room, the table, our half-eaten meal.

We run down the front path. Sylvie is watching us go from the upstairs window. Papa looks back when I point to her, and he motions to her to follow, but she just turns away. Aunt Sophie has convinced her that the police will not take women and children. Maman is pushing me along. I want her to stop pushing me, but she keeps telling me to hurry. The train will be leaving in five minutes, she says. If we are not on it, we will be caught. I start laughing. I have never seen my parents run before, and they are carrying heavy bags that weigh them down. "Hush, Ruth!" Maman says. "Hush!"

When we turn the corner, we pass Uncle Heinrich's apartment. Papa looks up at the shuttered window, but we must not yell. We must not draw attention. There's no sign of Monsieur Lambert in the street. Has he already warned Uncle Heinrich? Is he up there now, in the apartment, helping them get ready?

We hurry on. Soon, we come to the railroad station. We're lucky. The tracks are close to Uncle Heinrich's apartment. He should be coming any minute. But Uncle Heinrich does not come. Maman is looking all around. Papa takes his hat off and holds it in his hand. He is just staring up the street. We hear the train coming up the track. Cool air blows into my face as it passes us.

Papa looks back for Uncle Heinrich, but there is no sign of him in the street.

"Are we going to get caught, Maman?" I ask.

"Hush, Renée. When the train stops, get on right behind me. Do not say a word."

I nod. I know what to do. We've done this before, Maman and I. We stand on the platform, and we're in the middle of a cluster of people. The train pulls in and the conductor gets off. A station master calls out the train's destination. Papa has to show some papers to a man in uniform. We get on one of the last cars. It's hot inside the train. Maman and I look for Uncle Heinrich one last time, through the smeared windows. He's still not here. There is no one.

We find a space by the window. Maman and I sit down,

but Papa has to stand. He slides the bags onto the luggage rack over our heads. It's evening and the sky grows darker and I know Uncle Heinrich will be swallowed up in the dark. Maman and Papa just look at each other, saying nothing. If they talk about it, people around us will know we are Jewish, that we are running away.

I stare out the window. Luckily for us, the train is going to Albi, just as Monsieur Lambert said. Maman says we will go to the village called St. Juéry. She has the address where Aunt Hanna lives. It is written on the back of an envelope. The trees, the grass, the platform are slipping backward. The train starts slowly, but then it moves faster. If it would stop moving, only for a few moments, I know Uncle Heinrich could reach us in time.

When I turn away from the window, Maman is crying. She holds a handkerchief to her eyes. It makes me cry to watch her. We're long past the station. Papa lifts his hands and lets them fall. He means that there is nothing more he can do.

"Perhaps there will be another train," Papa mutters to Maman.

"*Non*." Maman shakes her head. "I heard a woman say it is the last train leaving tonight, so Monsieur Lambert was right."

"Where are we going to stay tonight, Maman?"

"With Uncle Oscar," she says, "at his house."

Papa looks at his watch. "It's eight-forty," he says. The train is moving fast now, rocking back and forth. It makes a pounding noise under my feet. I see a light in the window of one of the houses going by. Even I know that the lights are forbidden at night. Maybe it's the flashlight of a member of the French police, come to take away more Jews. Why do they hate us so? Why are they after us? I wish Jeannette were here, so that I could ask her. I never talk about this with my parents; I am too afraid of what they will say.

The sky is deepest blue, almost dark now, and there are shadows all around us. Soon, all the streets are gone and there is just the darkness. I can make out the hills, green in the daytime, and trees that lean over the tracks looking like dark ghosts. Maman says, "Oh, Benno! I forgot the blanket!" But then she shakes her head and looks back out the window; it is a silly thing.

After a while, Maman falls asleep, but I don't sleep. I watch the people who get on and off the train. The train is full of civilians. The man across from me gets up to leave, and Papa is able to sit down. I want to stay awake in case something happens. I keep thinking Uncle Heinrich is in the other car and will come through the doors any minute. Papa, too, keeps looking behind us whenever the door opens. Papa says the train will not stop again for a long time. "Try to get a little sleep, Renée," he says. He looks out the window. I can tell he is very sad. The train goes faster, it seems, following the curve of a rocky hillside. Then there is an open field.

I start to cry again. I remember I let Jeannette have my bracelet tonight, the one I found on the floor in school last week. She looked so pretty wearing it. She also borrowed my collection of ribbons. Papa says they will help Jeannette to remember me until we can be together again.

Maman's head nods from side to side as the train slows down. A conductor walks through the car and says the train will be stopping soon. Papa looks at his watch, and Maman opens her eyes. "It can't be Albi already," she says.

Papa shakes his head. "It's not."

The train rocks a little, following the curve of a blue-black field. It's as if we're gliding. Then there is the screech of the brakes, a train whistle sounds. Papa doesn't know where we are.

The man in the uniform steps into our car. "Last stop tonight. Everybody off the train!"

"He must be mistaken," Maman says. "This can't be Albi. What if it's a trick, Benno? Here we are in the middle of nowhere."

We have to get off. Papa reaches for our bags. Maman takes hold of my hand. We wait for the train to come to a stop, and then we move to the door. People are pushing behind us: everyone wants to know what is happening.

Outside, it's completely dark. We step onto the grass and the man in the uniform tells us we are outside of Albi. We will have to walk into the town. The train won't go any farther, but we don't know why. "Turn right up ahead," the man says, "and follow the main road." I hear people grumbling and complaining, but everyone starts walking in the same direction, along the dirt road. No one knows why the train won't go any farther.

Papa turns around several times. He tells me to walk in front of him. He tells Maman he's afraid that they are going to shoot us all in the back. He has heard of such things happening in other countries.

I've never been out in the night like this, except when Maman and I first arrived in Toulouse. I am frightened, but I don't show it to my parents. All around us, I hear the crickets and other strange sounds I've never heard before. Maman is holding my hand. In the darkness above our heads, I see strange black shapes swooping and soaring. Papa says they are just night birds, or bats. "But they won't hurt us, Ruth." He calls me by my real name. It doesn't matter anymore. No one is listening.

"How will we find St. Juéry now?" Maman wonders.

After a time, we come to a town. Some of the people walking ahead turn off into different streets. Papa calls, "Which way to St. Juéry, friend?" For a moment, there is no sound. I see a tiny orange light; it burns bright and then fades. I smell the scent of strong tobacco. It's someone smoking. I remember hearing a friend of Papa's say cigarettes are very hard to come by nowadays. A man's voice says, "Follow this road toward the center of town. When you come to the main street, turn left, and follow the Avenue Gambetta out of town."

"How long will it take us?"

"A good hour and a half from here, maybe longer with the little one."

Maman groans, but Papa says we have to make it to St. Juéry tonight. There is no turning back.

"It's easy for you," Maman says. "You've been in the Legion."

"Look, I'll carry all the bags," Papa offers. "We can't spend the night along the road, and what else have we got but time?"

Long after all the others have left the road, we are still walking. Sometimes Maman just stops and leans against the side of a building. The strange noises scare me. Perhaps they are animals calling to each other in the trees. Sometimes, we hear a twig snap by the side of the road and Papa just stops to listen. When we reach the main avenue, I can see the outline of a huge building in the distance. It has a curved tower, and a wall surrounds it. Papa says it is a cathedral. Maman says, "We could sleep there, inside the cathedral, tonight," but we turn left instead and follow the directions the man gave us.

"The cathedral is probably locked from the inside," Papa observes.

Maman does not say anything. Our shoes clomp along the road. I am so tired, Papa has to carry me. Maman takes the bags. Her feet hurt.

"Let's walk in the middle of the street," she says. "Maybe someone will come along in a car and pick us up."

We move out into the street and continue walking. Sometimes, Papa walks ahead of Maman, with me in his arms; sometimes, we are all together.

"Maybe this is not so smart," he says. "If anyone drives by this time of night, it would be the police. This would be a good way to get caught. Let's get back on the side of the road."

Maman is tired and doesn't want to walk anymore. Papa puts me down, and Maman sits on one of the bags in the middle of the street. "This is how it was in Alençon when we arrived," she murmurs. "I'm just glad you're here this time," she tells

Papa. "How will we ever find Oscar's house at this time of night? We have the address, but what if we can't find the street?"

Papa just shrugs. "There's sure to be someone walking by."

We are walking again. The darkness seems deeper. The black things are swooping down at me, and I put my hands up to keep them away. Papa lifts me up again and carries me. Maman takes the two bags. I am almost asleep in Papa's arms.

We follow the road until we see buildings in the distance. Maman says Oscar might be using another name. "Maybe they have false papers," she says. She stands for a moment in the middle of the road, resting. Papa says, "The sooner we get there, the sooner we can rest." He puts me down again, and I have to walk so he can carry the bags for Maman. Poor Maman; she is so tired, she starts crying. She covers her face with her hands. Papa puts the bags down again, and puts his arms around Maman, pulling her close. I walk over to them, my two parents, and I try to wrap my arms around their legs. Papa starts laughing, and then Maman.

Following the main street up a hill, we come to an intersection. There are buildings on either side of the street, all of them dark. At the top of the hill, there is a café on the corner, but it is closed. We walk over to it, and lean against the brick ledge while Maman takes out the crumpled piece of paper with Uncle Oscar's address written on it.

Fortunately for us, there is an old map of the town of St. Juéry pasted to the front window of the café. Papa lights a match in order to see better, and he traces his finger along the various streets shown on the map. He burns his finger and has to light another match. The air is so still and hot it feels as if it is midday. Maman leans against the window of the café. "You remember Uncle Oscar?" she asks me. "Your cousin, Raymonde?" I shake my head. "Don't worry. You will remember them when you see them." Maman smiles. Her eyes look tired; her face is drawn. She wipes her forehead with an old scarf she has been wearing around her neck.

"Here it is!" Papa says. "It's this way." He picks up our bags. "We have to walk back down the hill the way we came."

"*Oh, mon Dieu!*" Maman says. She is so tired, Papa has to help her up. We walk back down the street. I am so used to the dark now, I am not even afraid. When we reach the bottom of the hill, Papa stops and says, "Here. We turn up this street." Maman looks at him. "It should be along here," he says, "this row of houses."

We stop before a house that is set back from the street, and Papa walks up the path to the door. Maman and I follow. Everything is dark. There is no light in any of the windows. Blackout curtains here, too. Papa puts the bags down and knocks on the door. There is no sound. Maman's hand is on my shoulder.

"It's late, Benno. They must be asleep. Knock again."

So Papa knocks again, but no one comes. He goes around to the back of the house, and Maman and I follow. In the dark, I can see a fence surrounding a small garden, a wash line for laundry. Someone must live here. The crickets are loud, but no one sees them. They're like us; they hide in the night. Papa knocks at the narrow back door. He taps loudly on the glass window, even though it's painted over in dark blue.

Then, finally, there is a noise, a faint rustling inside. Footsteps are coming to the door. We wait in the middle of the night, with no idea of who will answer the door. Uncle Oscar and Aunt Hanna may have left a long time ago. But the door opens a few inches, and there is a tall man standing there, holding an oil lamp only very dimly lit. Maman whispers, "Oscar?" and the man comes closer to see better. He is squinting at us. I hear a sound come from Maman's throat, as though she is about to cry.

"Lissy?" the man says.

He is hurrying us inside the dark house, and Maman embraces him tearfully. He is her brother, and he is still alive and safe.

The Raid at Uncle Oscar's

Fortunately for us, Albi was on the direct line from Toulouse. That night, in August of 1942, the train went no farther. Albi was literally the last stop, and, for reasons unknown to us, the train stopped short of the station. Uncle Oscar pieced all of this together as Maman tried to tell him, all at once, everything that had happened. Papa sat silent and haggard-looking in a far corner of the dimly lit room. His face was ashen. Maman told Uncle Oscar about the neighbor who worked in the Préfecture, of how he had warned us of the impending roundup.

"We don't know what happened to Heinrich," Maman said quietly. "He never came to the station."

Uncle Oscar looked at Papa hopefully. "Perhaps there was another train, after yours, going in another direction?" he suggested.

"No." Papa shook his head. "The man from the Préfecture said it was the last train leaving tonight."

Uncle Oscar nodded and was silent. I stared at him for a

while, vaguely recalling the man who had looked so much younger the last time I saw him. His dark hair was thinning, and his skin was very tan, as if he had been working outside most of the time. To me, Uncle Oscar and Maman did not look alike. He was much taller than she; he had a broad face and dark hair, while Maman's face was long and rather narrow, and she had light brown hair.

Aunt Hanna came into the room and talked of other things. When I heard her voice, I did remember her, although she had lost weight and looked very tired. She had warmed tea for us, and there was also some bread and cheese. Maman laughed a little as she told Aunt Hanna that we had not even finished our dinner that evening.

"There was our supper, spread out on the table in our apartment, the food still hot, as Papa ushered us out the door."

"What a feast that will make for those policemen!" Papa joked.

We were sitting in a small room, just off the kitchen. Our faces looked unnaturally pale in the dim candlelight. It was so late, we all had dark circles under our eyes. I remember an upholstered chair and an old, overstuffed sofa under the window. The furniture had been left in the apartment by the previous occupants.

There were blackout curtains at all the windows, and Uncle Oscar explained that he could not turn on the light, for fear of attracting attention to the house. The Lyon family, also Jewish refugees, lived above Uncle Oscar and Aunt Hanna, and had known their share of trouble before their arrival in St. Juéry. They had experienced several close calls and were not taking any more chances in the new village. Uncle Oscar and the Lyons had agreed on the precautions they would take in order to draw as little attention to the house as possible. No lights on at night was the most important one.

Uncle Oscar told Papa that there were people in the village

who had ways of finding out what might have happened to Uncle Heinrich, or at least to the people in our building in Toulouse.

"Yes." Papa nodded. "There was a group like that in Toulouse. One or two of them lived in our building—mostly young men, but a few young women were involved, too. They always seemed to know what was going on before everyone else."

Uncle Oscar leaned forward. "Here, there are some young men, both in St. Juéry and in Arthès, who have helped us enormously. They have to work in secret, because otherwise they would be arrested and sent to work in the German labor camps. That is why they are resisting. I will contact one of them, and we will see what he can find out. He has a certain friend in Albi who goes to Toulouse once a month—"

"Eventually," Papa said in a low voice, "I will have to go back to Toulouse myself and try to find Heinrich. If I can't find him, I will look for Sophie and Jeannette. Sophie will be able to tell us what went wrong."

"Benno!" Maman cried. "You are not thinking! They could try to arrest you the moment you got off the train in Toulouse."

"He is my brother," Papa said emphatically.

There was an awkward silence. Aunt Hanna looked toward the doorway and smiled. "Ruth," she said, "here is someone I think you will remember."

My cousin Raymonde was standing there in the doorway. I had not seen her in two years. She had heard voices and come out to see who had arrived at such a late hour. Shyly we said hello to each other, and Raymonde led me into the bedroom to see her sister, Evelyne. I remembered Raymonde's baby sister, but now she was almost three years old. "She still doesn't know how to talk," Raymonde told me. Evelyne slept with a bottle at night; her small fingers were wrapped around it, and with her other hand, she clung to a frayed blanket. She was sound asleep. Raymonde laughed at her. "She's such a baby," she said.

There were only three rooms in the apartment: a bedroom, the kitchen, and the sitting room. Each room was small and cramped. There was little space to walk around. The ceiling was low, and Uncle Oscar had to stoop when entering the sitting room from the kitchen. A side stairway on the outside of the building led to the upstairs apartment, where the Lyon family lived. Uncle Oscar said that their floor plan was similar to his. You could tell that the furniture in Uncle Oscar's apartment was old, and the carpet with its rose-patterned center was worn and frayed. The flowered wallpaper was stained and peeling in places; bits of plaster rained down in a powder whenever someone with heavy footsteps walked across the floor. There was no running water, and everyone had to use the outhouses in the back. The building had been closed up for some time before Uncle Oscar had arrived there; thus, the furniture, the woodwork, and even the floorboards were warped or mildewy.

Aunt Hanna told me I could sleep with Raymonde in the bedroom. Maman and Papa were to sleep in the sitting room. It was the middle of the night, and we were so tired no one could talk anymore. Aunt Hanna told us we must rest. "In the morning, we'll make plans," she told Maman. "I'm so glad we're together again, Lissy."

In the garden out back, Aunt Hanna grew vegetables. In the afternoons, Raymonde and I would stand out there, take a hose, and spray each other with the cool water. At night, we would steal Evelyne's bottle and give her one of our cups. She never protested, but seemed to prefer drinking out of the cup while Raymonde and I laughed and pretended to be babies, drinking from the bottle. I loved playing games with Raymonde. I was happy to have someone my own age to play with, although I still thought of Jeannette and missed her.

During that first week after our arrival in St. Juéry, Papa and Uncle Oscar made plans. Uncle Oscar promised Papa that he would try to find someone who might be going to Toulouse in the next few weeks. "It may be," he told Papa, "that your brother went to another 'safe house.' Perhaps he just didn't want to leave Toulouse. Or perhaps he tried but missed the train, and had no choice but to hide out somewhere else until he could get word to his wife."

"I've thought of these possibilities myself," Papa agreed. "But there's a feeling I have. A bad feeling."

Maman and Aunt Hanna exchanged glances as they stood drying dishes at the basin in the kitchen. Aunt Hanna would draw water at the pump out back, and then, with a large bucket, she would bring it in and fill the basin. She usually washed, while Maman would dry the dishes.

No one brought up the subject of Uncle Heinrich for the rest of that week.

We lived on vegetables from Aunt Hanna's garden, as well as potatoes and leek soup. Maman sold a small silver Shabbat candlestick, one of the ones she and Papa had used for the Sabbath prayer until their arrival in France, in order to buy veal on the black market. It was her way of thanking Uncle Oscar and Aunt Hanna for taking care of us during those first days in St. Juéry.

We went to bed early in the country.

One night we were awakened at 3:00 A.M. by the sound of a truck pulling to a stop out in the street. Doors slammed, and I heard the sound of heavy boots walking across the square stones. A man's voice shouted, "Lyon! Monsieur Lyon!" Someone pounded on the false door in the front of the building. Within minutes, Uncle Oscar and Papa had us all out of bed and standing by the back door. I clung to Maman. Aunt Hanna held Evelyne close so that she would not cry. Raymonde and I held hands.

The police discovered the side door leading up to the

second floor apartment. The next sounds were those of the door being forced open. We heard the police rushing up the wooden stairs. They went right past the wall of the sitting room as we huddled in the darkness. Their voices were loud and angry. They were French police, and they kept shouting, "Lyon! Lyon!"

We stood, motionless, like marble figures, as furniture was turned over and doors were opened and slammed shut above our heads. They banged another door, probably the door to the bedroom, which could have been locked from the inside to slow the police down. An object fell to the floor and shattered. We heard no screams or crying, no voices other than those of the police. Then the boots returned down the steps. Now it was our turn to be caught, I thought. They would come around to the back of the house and find the narrow door. Uncle Oscar whispered, "When I give the signal, we will run down the stairs, one by one, into the garden. Wait until the person ahead of you has made it to the garden before you dart out. Get as far away from the house as possible. Scatter, like birds, and then sink down into the dirt. Do not make a sound. Do not scream or cry."

I turned my head and buried it in Maman's skirt. Then I heard the click as Uncle Oscar opened the back door. But no one moved. We did not have to, because they never called Uncle Oscar's name. They did not even come to the apartment door. Uncle Oscar cautioned us with a whisper, "Don't move yet. It could be a trap." Or could they have come only for the Lyons?

We waited in the dark kitchen for several more minutes until we heard the truck engine starting up. Papa and Uncle Oscar went to the window and pulled back the blackout curtain as the truck pulled away. I could not see Papa's face in the dark, but he shook his head back and forth. Coming away from the window, he said, "That truck was filled with people from the village."

We all looked at each other, hardly breathing.

"Oscar," Maman whispered, "why didn't they call your name?"

"We are probably not yet on the lists. They don't know we are here."

"And the Lyons?" Papa asked.

"They escaped."

"*Vraiment* [Truly]? How can you tell?"

"When I was standing by the door, I heard someone in the garden. They must have jumped out of the upstairs window, swung onto the big branch of the walnut tree, dropped to the ground, and run away."

"Where will they go?"

"Into the fields for tonight. After that, probably to Marseille or Nice."

Although this was not the first roundup my parents had witnessed, it was the closest we had come thus far to being taken away. We crept back to bed, but I slept with Maman the rest of that night, too frightened to leave her. I was afraid the police might return for us. "First Heinrich, now this," Maman muttered to Papa that night. "How can we possibly get through another year?"

It dawned on me for the first time that night that Maman and Papa actually believed Uncle Heinrich had been arrested and taken away. I tried to imagine how it had been, the police coming up the stairs, pounding on Uncle Heinrich's door; but I couldn't bear to imagine any more. I wouldn't let myself. I never stopped hoping that my parents were wrong.

A week later, a man known to Uncle Oscar only by the name Bernard found a one-room apartment for us in Arthès, the neighboring village just across the Tarn River. We lived on a side street, above the village *tabac,* or tobacco shop. Our apartment was below that of the Fedou family in the same building; they were to be our protectors. We did not realize, when we first met the Fedous, that they had hidden another

Jewish family in the very apartment we were about to inhabit. The night the roundups had occurred in St. Juéry, this family was among the first to be taken. The Fedous had felt terrible, blaming themselves for having failed to protect the family that had been entrusted to them. This time, it would be different. They were determined to be zealous in guarding us.

The Fedous were Catholics, and therefore had nothing to fear, at least on the surface, from the French police. But they were risking their lives in order to give us shelter. It was common knowledge that any citizen who was caught harboring Jews would be arrested on the spot and sent, along with the Jews, to a concentration camp. Monsieur Fedou eventually would become a member of a Resistance network that operated throughout the Southern Zone. My parents learned, long after our arrival there, that almost every young man in the village was a member of a Resistance group, or was able to help the Resistance fighters in some way.

We became very fond of the Fedous, and I loved playing with their daughter, Andrée, who became something of a replacement for Jeannette to me. She was about fifteen years old when we met. She was small-boned and thin, with blue eyes, brown hair, and a good sense of humor. That year, her older sister, Lucette, was engaged to be married. I thought Lucette was very pretty; she had brown hair and an open, gentle face. Madame Fedou was a kind, good-natured woman. She was short and rather stocky, and she wore her already-white hair short around her ruddy-complexioned face. Monsieur Fedou was also heavy and always dressed in old peasant denims that had a noticeable patina to them. I thought Monsieur Fedou never changed his clothes; he was always wearing his blue overalls, a vest, the watch he carried on an old gold chain, and a béret. He had a mustache and graying hair; and, more than anything else, I remember how he loved garlic. In my mind I always see him bent over, knife in hand, peeling a garlic clove. There were many evenings when we gathered in the Fedous' cluttered dining room to play and would finally settle into chairs around the big table and listen to the grown-ups talk about the war.

Arthès was a small village filled with steep, narrow streets and short buildings with red-tiled roofs. The *tabac* overlooked the main square, while the entrance to our apartment faced the side street that ran perpendicular to the Place du Village. Hidden behind these narrow village houses were beautiful vegetable and flower gardens; and beyond the village, in the distance, were the fields where many of the men from the village worked. People crossed from Arthès into St. Juéry each day to shop or to catch a ride on the charcoal-burning taxi that occasionally came from Albi to take someone into town. Unless it was an emergency, however, there was little transportation available to and from the two villages, apart from bicycling and walking. Fortunately, although we lived across the river from St. Juéry, we were able to see Uncle Oscar's family fairly regularly. As Jews in hiding, however, we spent little time out in the open.

I accompanied Papa one afternoon to see Uncle Oscar. Papa would not rest until he could return to Toulouse and try to contact Aunt Sophie. He began to outline a plan, while Uncle Oscar listened and nodded.

"While we were in Toulouse," he began, "we heard, by word-of-mouth, about an organization that would look after children and place them in special homes in the event that something happened to us. It is called the O.S.E. [Oeuvre de Secours aux Enfants]. Our neighbor, who worked in the Préfecture de Police, told us about an office building where we could go to find out more information. Well, I went there one day, and talked to a very nice woman. She herself was Jewish and knew that there were many like us in Toulouse who were terrified by all the roundups in the surrounding neighborhoods. I told her that if anything should happen, Lissy and I would go to St. Juéry, since we knew you were already here. This woman looked in her files and gave us the name of a Monsieur Harlam, who is one of the directors of this organization. He heads an office in St. Juéry, but lives in Arthès."

"Very good. Do you have the address?"

Papa nodded. "The woman said he may also be able to provide us with some money to get by, although it would have to be a secret exchange. That's how they operate."

"What about false papers? If you're going back to Toulouse, you'll need false papers," Uncle Oscar reminded Papa.

Papa shrugged. "I'm not sure about that."

"Well, if this man can't provide them, I know a man in the village—"

The next day, Papa met with Monsieur Harlam. He was able to obtain enough money to make his way back to Toulouse. The man could not provide Papa with false papers, however, unless Papa would agree to wait several weeks. Papa could not wait. Uncle Oscar reassured Papa, and they agreed to apply for false papers through another source: Uncle Oscar's friend who lived in St. Juéry.

That evening, I went with Papa to an old office building on a narrow side street in St. Juéry, not far from the local mayor's office. It was after six o'clock. Papa gave the impression that he was just out for a walk with his little girl. Uncle Oscar joined us at the entrance to a café, not far from the office building. When he saw me, he raised his eyebrows.

"Benno! Why did you bring the little one?" he asked. "Weren't you afraid to risk it?"

"I thought that bringing Renée along would put to rest any suspicions people might have about what we're doing here," Papa said quietly.

Papa and Uncle Oscar talked of unimportant things. After a while, Uncle Oscar nonchalantly glanced at his watch. Since he knew the man we were about to see, he told us to follow him, in five minutes, into the building. He would go in first, talk to the man, and make sure that there would be no trouble, nor unexpected interruptions. Papa and Uncle Oscar laughed together, enjoying the mystery, but then Uncle Oscar's face became very grave. We watched him as he walked over to the office building, entered, and signaled to us from inside the door that we should leave if anyone began to watch us or give us suspicious glances.

When five minutes had passed without incident, Papa led me toward the office building. We entered the building and climbed a narrow flight of steps. Then we walked along a corridor until we came to the end of the dark hall, where there was a narrow door. Papa knocked, and the door opened at once. Uncle Oscar was standing there, waiting for us. He hurried us inside. A short, burly man was sitting at a desk with his back to us. He said, "Welcome," and that was all. A cigarette was smoldering in an ashtray on the man's desk. Papa asked where he got the cigarettes, since the shortage was getting worse, but the man did not answer. There was little light in the room, and no place to sit. Books were scattered about, and the sparse furniture was covered with strange folders, notebooks, and timetables. The man worked in the mayor's office, doubling in his spare time as a forger of false papers for the Jewish people who were in hiding.

"This is the man," said Uncle Oscar pointing to Papa. "He needs false papers for his wife and his little girl, but especially for himself."

"What are the names?" The man remained at his desk, hardly turning his head to address us. We realized later that he did not want us to have a close look at him, so that we would not be able to identify him if we were ever caught by the police.

Papa answered him. "Benno Kapp, Elisabeth Kapp, and Ruth Kapp."

"My name is Renée!" I blurted.

"Good." The man laughed. "You're ahead of the game. You can keep that name, since it's a good French name." To Papa, he said, "Look, I will change your name, but I have to keep the same initials, if possible."

Papa agreed.

The man thought for a moment, then consulted a notebook. "Let's see," he said, "what about Bernard Kappère?"

"*Oui.*" Papa nodded. "That sounds good."

"Well." The man hesitated. "I'm not sure. It's too similar to one I just did last week. I'll change it to a 'c.' Bernard Caper."

Uncle Oscar said that would do. The man held out his hand, and Papa gave him an envelope that contained the money. Then the man consulted a large, heavy book. He turned several pages. He was studying a map.

"I'll put down Bissheim, how's that?" he asked. "No." He paused, changing his mind again.

"Wittenheim?" Uncle Oscar suggested.

"Yes, that's good. You were all born in Alsace, as of tonight. I hope your French is adequate, because, as of this moment, you're a Frenchman."

Papa smiled. The man finally turned around and looked straight at me. "Remember, little one. You have a new last name. You're a new person. Don't go getting your papa into trouble."

I shook my head. We were told the papers would be ready in only a few days. Uncle Oscar would arrange to pick up the papers as soon as he had heard from the man that they were ready.

In a short time, we were walking back down the steps of the office building. The smell of the musty, smoke-filled room was behind us. "Renée Caper," I said to myself. I couldn't decide whether I liked my new name or not. I would go to a new school in the village and I would be a new person. I had always thought of myself as French, but there had been constant reminders that I was also a Jewish child: the

Papa's false identification card with the French name, Bernard Caper, that he used to hide his German-Jewish identity.

roundups, the suspicious looks, the fear. Now, all that had been erased. I was not Jewish. I was going to be protected by a false piece of identification, a lie. My new name would save me from the police, that was what Maman had told me.

"Why does he do that for us?" Papa asked Uncle Oscar on the way home.

"Why? Because he is against the Pétain regime," Oscar said under his breath. "But he needs his job to survive. It's as simple as that."

I did not understand. How could all of these people be against our Marshal? There were posters everywhere of the Marshal; he was supposed to be a hero. Was the Marshal against us? I soon came to believe that Jeannette perhaps had been right about Pétain. The victor of Verdun had begun to take on the suspicious character of the old man who stared back at me from all the posters in St. Juéry. He hardly resembled the man I had glimpsed in Toulouse, waving from an open car.

"Papa, will we be able to find Uncle Heinrich now?" I asked when we got home that night.

"Yes," he told me. "Someday soon."

I started going to the village school. That was when I truly missed Jeannette the most. There was no one to walk home with me. Evelyne and Raymonde went to school in St. Juéry, so I was all alone and scared in the strange environment. The worst part was having to face all the children at the new school on my own. Even Maman could not walk me to school; it would have been too dangerous.

At that time, the schoolhouse in Arthès was only one large room. There were rows of wooden tables with benches where we sat to do our lessons. The teacher's desk stood on a platform in the front, and there was a wood-burning stove in the center that kept us comfortably warm in the winter. It was impossible to lose oneself in that room. If you forgot your books, or your lessons were incomplete, the entire school knew about it.

As was the case with all the village children, I had little to wear. Maman would spend hours unraveling sweaters, and then she would knit dresses for me out of the old yarn. She sewed clothes out of old linens or any scraps of material she could find in the village.

"It's hard to believe I am reduced to this," she once said to Papa as she hemmed a dress for me. "In our shop in Germany, we had bolts and bolts of all of those beautiful fabrics piled high to the ceiling."

Papa did not say anything. I could tell he kept the sadness and anger buried deep inside. He would just look at Maman and then turn away.

Papa was able to find work in a local factory that produced knives. The factory Sauts du Tarn was situated between the two villages, just on the outskirts of St. Juéry, before crossing the bridge. Papa's shift ran from six in the morning until two-thirty in the afternoon. He was usually home when I returned from school, and I was able to forget the loneliness I had felt all morning as soon as he began to tell me stories about Morocco.

We had ration cards, and we had to take them with us when we went to get food. Maman and I stood in line for various products. It seemed we ate the same foods all the time. Although my parents had observed the kosher food laws before the war, it was practically impossible for them to continue to do so. They were thankful to get any kind of meat in 1942. You could get veal on the black market. Lungs and heart were not rationed, but not very palatable either. We could not bring ourselves to eat them.

One afternoon Uncle Oscar came up the stairs and knocked on the door to our apartment. He had news for Papa. My parents sat down with Uncle Oscar at the table, and he told them about a Protestant minister in the area who made frequent trips to the Red Cross center in Toulouse. The minister was a member of an organization that helped Jewish families who were in hiding. The minister had told Uncle Oscar that he would certainly accompany Papa to Toulouse; he would pose as Papa's uncle. In a few weeks, the minister would be making another trip to Toulouse, and Papa would accompany him then. They would leave very early in the morning, and Papa was not to forget his false identity papers.

Papa's face brightened. He agreed to the plan wholeheartedly.

"It could be extremely dangerous, Benno," Uncle Oscar warned.

"What isn't these days?" Papa said, smiling.

Uncle Oscar agreed to take Papa to see the minister the following evening, so that they could make the final arrangements. After that, it was simply a matter of waiting for the day when Papa could finally return to Toulouse. Unfortunately, Papa's positive mood waned the more he thought about the trip he would soon make. He feared that whatever news he learned would be grim.

PART TWO: IN HIDING

September 1942 to August 1944

It is such a secret place, the land of tears.
—Antoine de Saint-Exupéry

Arrest

I have not seen Papa in two days. He is in Toulouse, looking for Uncle Heinrich and Aunt Sophie. Before he left, Maman was upset, trying to persuade him to abandon his search. Papa was especially on edge, wondering when he'd receive word that it was the right time to go to Toulouse.

I imagine all sorts of things. The one daydream I keep having is of Papa coming through the door with Uncle Heinrich, Aunt Sophie, and Jeannette clustered around him. I imagine myself running over to them and burying myself in Uncle Heinrich's embrace. I can hear him laughing, and I smell that scent of the pine forest all over my uncle's coat. Then Jeannette takes me in her arms and hugs me. I cannot imagine beyond that; there is only that fleeting moment in my mind of a happiness that is just beyond my reach.

When Papa really does come through the door, he is very much alone. I want to ask, "Are they all right?" "Is Jeannette safe?" "Did she ask for me?" As he tries to tell us, I see everything happening as if I am there. I am afraid, the way I used to be in Toulouse.

*   *   *

Papa and the minister step off the train in Toulouse. Papa expects to see a city emptied of its population, a city with abandoned buildings, homes, and stores. Instead, he finds Toulouse relatively unchanged. If anything, there are more people; there is more hunger, more isolation and fear. He is especially aware of the large numbers of children roaming the streets, searching for their parents or for some kind of safe shelter.

From the Red Cross center, Papa and the minister are directed to a narrow alley behind a row of houses. When they reach the tall dilapidated building in the center of the alley, Papa goes up to the door and knocks. Almost at once, the door opens. Papa speaks to an elderly woman, who points up the stairs. The minister promises to wait just inside the doorway, and Papa hurries up to the first floor.

He knocks on the door. After several minutes, he turns away, assuming that Aunt Sophie is not there, but just then the door opens. Jeannette lets Papa in. They embrace and say a few words of greeting to each other, but nothing more. For Papa, it is as if they have only just seen each other the night before, as if all the agonizing days and weeks have never been. Jeannette leads Papa through the small room into a narrow passageway that serves as a kitchen. That is when he sees Aunt Sophie standing there, her back to him, looking out the window. She is staring at nothing in particular. As soon as she turns and sees him, she lets out a cry and covers her mouth as the tears come. Papa goes to her and kisses her, once on each cheek.

"Oh, Benno—!" she says.

"How is Heinrich?"

"Benno, he is not here."

"Tell me."

They sit down in the kitchen, and it's as if I'm there, too, listening to the story. Aunt Sophie wipes her eyes with her apron as she begins to tell Papa what happened.

It is the night we left Toulouse.

They are in the middle of the Sabbath dinner. Jeannette's friend, Malcolm, has come; he is telling how he and some friends from school sabotaged what they think was a Nazi supply wagon passing through Toulouse. Not even the teachers at school have found out what Jeannette's friend has done. Aunt Sophie is not sure that she believes that the boy and his friends would be smart enough or courageous enough to do such a thing, or even that a Nazi supply wagon actually passed through the city, but she does not express her doubts. After all, the boy is really just trying to impress Jeannette. There are many Jewish boys in the area who talk about forming a clandestine group. Jeannette, smiling all the time, is very proud of her friend.

Just as they finish dinner, there is a knock at the door. It is not trouble, because it is the secret knock. Jeannette goes to the door. A dark-haired man is standing there. He is out of breath.

"I've been sent to warn you," the man says. "There is going to be a roundup. Any minute now. Your brother, Monsieur Kapp, has already been warned and sent me to tell you. He has already left the apartment. A train is leaving for Albi tonight. If you're fast, you can catch it."

Uncle Heinrich has never seen the man before and doesn't know whether to believe him. Aunt Sophie mentions that this is the man who has helped Lissy and Ruth, but Uncle Heinrich seems hardly to be listening. There is no time to ask questions. In a moment, the man is gone. Uncle Heinrich and Jeannette's friend stand up. What should they do? "It's too late for the train," says Aunt Sophie. "We've got to hide."

"But if we hurry," Jeannette insists, "maybe we could meet Aunt Lissy and Uncle Benno at the station."

"No, we'll hide," Uncle Heinrich murmurs.

"We can't go downstairs," says Malcolm. "The police could be in the street already. We should go down the hall and hide in one of the empty storage rooms."

"That's stupid!" Jeannette cries. "Don't you think they'll look in there?"

But it's too late. Already, there are trucks screeching to a halt out in the street. Aunt Sophie freezes in terror. The doors to the truck slam shut, the boots are on the pavement.

"French police! Unlock the door!"

They are after Jewish men and members of some group that Aunt Sophie does not know. Any man found in the building will be arrested. Someone must have bolted the door at the bottom of the stairs from the inside, because the police have to break the door down.

"Out the window," Uncle Heinrich whispers. "We'll climb onto the roof and hide."

"No!" says Aunt Sophie. "You'll fall! It's too high!"

But Malcolm is out the window in no time, his legs disappearing, only his shoes visible as he climbs to the roof. He is very fast and used to this sort of thing. Just as the police break down the front door at the bottom of the stairs, Uncle Heinrich is out the window, standing on the ledge, then climbing up onto the roof. A pair of hands reaches down to help him up.

Aunt Sophie and Jeannette hurry back to the table, blow out the candles, and hide them. Doors below them are opened and then slammed shut. There are screams: women crying as their husbands are taken down to the waiting trucks. Jeannette hurries to the sink with the two extra plates and bowls; she hides them in a cupboard and takes two chairs away from the table. Aunt Sophie has hidden the glasses and utensils.

The police pound on their door. "Police! Open at once!" they shout.

Aunt Sophie looks around the room once more. Is there any sign of the men who were here moments before? She is breathing heavily; her heart is pounding, and she is afraid that they will see how terrified she is. She nods to Jeannette to open the door.

There are three of them: two policemen and a Frenchman wearing civilian clothes. He must be one of the informers. The policemen are wearing wide black belts. They come into the room and look everywhere for Uncle Heinrich.

"Where is your husband, Madame?" says the man wearing civilian clothes.

Aunt Sophie shrugs. "He was taken away two weeks ago, and I have not seen him or heard from him since then."

"Two weeks ago?" The men look at one another.

"Yes."

"That's a lie," says one of the policemen. "There was no roundup in this district two weeks ago."

"He was taken at work," says Jeannette.

"Where are your papers?"

Aunt Sophie walks slowly to the armoire. She opens the door and reaches for a packet of letters; among them are her papers and Jeannette's. As she turns around to hand them over to the man, she notices the gun in the holster of one of the policemen's belts. The other carries a club.

"Alsace, eh?" the man asks.

"Yes. We are from Alsace."

One of the men searches the room. He checks the closet, the alcove, under the bed. Another man leans out the window but sees nothing. He opens the armoire, where there are several books lined up on one of the shelves; among them is Uncle Heinrich's copy of *Le Petit Chaperon Rouge*. Hidden behind this row of books, at the back of the shelf, is Uncle Heinrich's book of letters to the Kapp family still in Germany. Aunt Sophie holds her breath as the policeman peruses the shelves of the armoire. She knows that if Uncle Heinrich's book is found, the police will learn everything. There is information about Uncle Oscar and Aunt Hanna, about Maman and Papa and me. The police would be able to trace our whereabouts, and eventually we would be rounded up. But the man turns away from the books and closes the door to the armoire.

"Good night, Madame," says the informer. "Enjoy your evening."

Then they are gone, back down the stairs. Jeannette runs to the window and looks out. Below her, in the street, she sees the trucks. They are filled with men from the building and the neighborhood. One of the men being led away catches sight of her just before the doors to the truck are slammed shut. She recognizes him. She has seen him sometimes talking to her friend. She wonders if Malcolm can see him, too, from where he crouches, on the roof. She knows the man lived several blocks away. What was he doing in the building? Will the police torture him? Will he give them all away?

The trucks start up and then drive off down the street. Aunt Sophie and Jeannette are hardly able to move. They sit at the table in silence for a long time, until it is fully dark. That is when they hear footsteps above their heads, on the roof. Within minutes, Uncle Heinrich and Jeannette's friend are back down in the room. Jeannette is laughing; they have outsmarted the police. She and Malcolm embrace. Aunt Sophie is in tears. But Uncle Heinrich says they must be practical now; they must think. They are not yet out of danger. He walks slowly back and forth. He wants to know what the police said, the questions they asked. Soon, Jeannette's friend must leave. Jeannette is worried, but he tells her he will be all right. She goes to the bottom of the stairs with him. When she comes back into the room, her parents are making plans. Aunt Sophie tells her, "We're leaving tomorrow, early."

Jeannette does not say anything. She knows now that she will never see her friend again. Uncle Heinrich says, "Benno and Lissy probably got on the train safely. They must have gone to Albi. Lissy's brother is there. In the morning, we'll go to the station and wait for the next train."

"Heinrich," Aunt Sophie murmurs, "do you think it's safe for us to stay here tonight?"

"I think so. Why would they return to a building where

there has just been a massive roundup? As far as they know, they caught all the Jewish men here tonight."

"What will happen to them?"

"First, they'll be taken to the Bureau de Police and questioned. Then—"

"A detention camp," Jeannette fills in. She knows the procedure as well as Uncle Heinrich.

"After that," Uncle Heinrich continues, "I do not know. No one does."

In the night, no one can sleep.

In just a few hours, they will be leaving. Uncle Heinrich wants everyone to be ready before sunrise. Aunt Sophie lies awake, her eyes wide, all night. Every sound in the street could be the police. She wants to nudge Uncle Heinrich to say, "Let's go now, what's the point of waiting until morning?" but she thinks he has just drifted off. She knows there are no trains running in the middle of the night. So she waits, and the hours go by slowly, and the room is hot and black and still. She listens to the rhythm of her husband's breathing.

In the morning, just before dawn, everyone is awake. Jeannette is dressing. They all pack what few possessions they have in a single bag. Aunt Sophie is already dressed, for she has been up for the last hour. Uncle Heinrich is standing at the sink, shaving. Before he has time to wipe the soap from his face, there is knocking at the door. Everyone stops, stands motionless. Uncle Heinrich and Aunt Sophie look at each other. It is all over.

There is pounding, and then the dreaded words again. "Open up! French Police!"

Uncle Heinrich himself opens the door, dabbing his face with a towel. His face is worried, the lines on his forehead deeper than usual. In seconds, they are all over the place, searching every corner of the room. The same men from the night before have come back. The man in civilian clothes is smiling. He looks as if he has slept in his clothes.

"Well, Monsieur Kapp," he says, "did you have a nice evening?"

"What do you want with him!" Aunt Sophie cries. "He has done nothing!" Her words fall on deaf ears.

"We will be taking you to the station, Monsieur Kapp. We must ask you a few questions."

"But he hasn't even finished shaving!" Aunt Sophie pleads. "He will have to pack some things. Give him a couple of hours at least—"

"Just bring your toilet articles," one of the policemen says. "You'll only be gone for a few hours."

Aunt Sophie begins to cry, clutching Uncle Heinrich's arm. She does not believe them.

Uncle Heinrich wipes the soap away from his face. Jeannette runs to him and kisses him, tears streaming down her face. She clings to him and sobs aloud, "Papa!" as though there were something he could do. Then Uncle Heinrich and Aunt Sophie embrace. When Aunt Sophie kisses her husband, she whispers something to him, but no one hears what she says.

"Come on," the policeman shouts. "Get moving!"

Just as they start toward the door, Jeannette rushes toward one of the policemen, but she is smacked in the face and thrown backward into the room. "You want to go along?" the informer asks.

The police lead Uncle Heinrich down the dark stairway, one in front, and one behind him. There is no chance of breaking away, of hitting one of them over the head and running. There is no way to escape.

Aunt Sophie follows Jeannette to the window. Both are sobbing. They see Uncle Heinrich being taken to the truck. There are several other men being led out of other buildings in the first light of morning. Uncle Heinrich looks up at the window one last time, but he cannot wave. His hands have been cuffed behind his back, as though he were a criminal.

As Aunt Sophie comes to the end of the story, Jeannette puts some bread and tea on the table. "We have not seen him since that morning," she tells Papa. "What will they do to him?"

Papa cannot answer; the tears have come to his eyes. He is remembering the night of our departure from Toulouse: how he had gone to Uncle Heinrich's apartment after work to share a bottle of wine with him. He remembers how Jeannette came into the room that evening to show off her new skirt. It had seemed to Papa, for those brief moments, that they were in another time, a place where there was no danger.

Aunt Sophie is slumped in her chair. "He fought in the Foreign Legion," she says. "Have they no respect for that?"

"Yes," Papa says. "He should not have been taken. I will do what I can to find out what they've done with him. I know someone who might be able to look into it for me. If Heinrich is still in France, he would be in one of the camps. Perhaps there has been some mistake and they were not aware of his status, that he fought in the Legion—" But Papa cannot go on. These are only words intended to comfort Aunt Sophie; he does not believe them himself. "In the meantime," he continues, "why don't you come back to Albi with me? There is room enough, and it will be much safer for you and Jeannette. We can all go back on the train together."

"No." Aunt Sophie shakes her head. She is adamant. "They've already got Heinrich. What's the point of hiding now? Besides, if he should get out, if he's still alive and he escapes somehow, or is released, how would he find us? If we stay here, he will have no trouble."

Papa nods. He takes a piece of paper and a pencil out of his pocket. He hesitates before writing down the name of our street in Arthès. He knows how dangerous it is to exchange such information, even with a member of one's own family. "Just in case you change your mind," he tells her, "this is the address."

"Benno!" Aunt Sophie cries, as though suddenly jolted out of her grief. "Are you crazy? Do you have any idea how dangerous this is? If the police should ever find this scrap of paper with your address . . . You should not even have come here in the first place. You were taking your life in your hands by leaving Arthès." She tears the scrap of paper into little pieces and throws them in the sink.

Papa turns away. He mutters, almost inaudibly, "How do you think it is for us to be separated from all of you? To wonder, for weeks on end, whether you're alive or dead? I had to come. It would be so much better if you came back with me to the village. Jeannette could go to school there with Renée. It would be far safer than to remain here."

"I cannot," Aunt Sophie mutters.

He leaves some money on the table. "Keep this for your mother," he tells Jeannette. "I'll come back as soon as it is possible, to see how you are getting along."

Papa stays in Toulouse with the minister until the next morning, when they return to the Red Cross center and then depart Toulouse for Albi. Before leaving the city, he pays another brief visit to Aunt Sophie. He is afraid he might not see her again. He kisses her goodbye and then turns to Jeannette, hugging her close. They follow him to the door.

"Try to convince your mother to join us in Arthès," he tells Jeannette. "You have to think of her safety and your own. At least we would all be together. I will try to find out all I can about your papa. I am so sorry, my dear. Take care of each other."

They embrace again. Papa goes back down the stairs, then follows the minister down the alley, through the streets, toward the station.

It takes Papa a long time to tell us the story. When he is finished, none of us speaks. There are tears in Papa's eyes; his brother has been taken away, and we do not know how to comfort him. In spite of what he told Jeannette, he knows there is very little he can do for Uncle Heinrich. "I always thought, if we could just stay ahead of the Germans, we would be all right," Papa says. "But the French are after us as well. How can we fight two enemies in the same country and still survive?"

I want to ask, Will Uncle Heinrich die? Will they kill him? But I don't dare say the words. Papa takes me on his lap and holds me close. I remember how Uncle Heinrich used to read to me as I sat on his lap, turning the pages in the book. Will he ever read to me again?

"Whatever happens," Maman says, "we must not think that way, Benno. We have to keep believing that he will be all right, and that we will, too. We have to believe that." She gets up from her chair to set the table.

Papa is silent. He has had no contact from the members of his family left behind in Germany. He wonders all the time what happened to them, and now Papa will not be able to stop himself from wondering each day what they have done to his brother. Will he, too, fade from our lives forever?

Later that afternoon, we went into St. Juéry for food. We stopped to visit Aunt Hanna and Uncle Oscar. There was another family there whom we had never met before. They were Monsieur and Madame Kahn, and they had two children, Emmy and Jean-Claude. The Kahns were Alsatian, and they had been sent, along with hundreds of other Alsatian Jews, to the south of France under Nazi orders.

I played out back in the garden with Raymonde and the new girl, Emmy, who was my age. Now I had two friends with whom to play. Emmy would be going to school with me in Arthès. We liked the same games. We ran around in circles and then fell to the ground. The last one to fall was out of the next game. Usually, Jean-Claude was out because he refused to stop running.

Uncle Oscar came out for a few moments to watch us. He had a camera in his hands. The camera belonged to Monsieur Kahn, but he told Uncle Oscar to take some pictures. Papa came outside, and Uncle Oscar took several pictures of us all. When Aunt Hanna came out to pick some of her vegetables for our dinner, Papa took a picture of Aunt Hanna, Uncle Oscar, and all of the children standing in the garden.

"Someday," Aunt Hanna commented, "when we're all free, we'll look at those pictures and try to forget how things were."

There was a lot to eat that night, only because everyone had contributed food. We sat down, and Uncle Oscar whispered the motzi, the prayer over the bread, before we ate. Emmy and I sat together. Everyone was solemn as Papa told the story of his trip to Toulouse. The sun had set, and the street seemed unnaturally quiet. When Papa said the word "arrested," Monsieur Kahn looked down at his plate and shook his head. He, too, had seen whole truckloads of Jews being taken away.

"Well," Madame Kahn said, "it's better than being taken away by the Gestapo."

"Oh, I'm not so sure it makes much difference anymore," Uncle Oscar disagreed.

Madame Kahn was murmuring, afraid that we children would hear too much of the conversation. "Well," she went on, "if you get caught, you get taken to these camps, and, while it's not pleasant—"

"You're naïve to believe that!" Papa cut in. "The Nazis have had these concentration camps for years—since well before the war. We can't imagine how atrocious the conditions are. You get treated like a prisoner of war, or worse. And the French camps are just as bad! I assure you, it is far from pleasant!"

For a moment, no one said anything. Papa was embarrassed for raising his voice, and Madame Kahn apologized for upsetting him. Aunt Hanna took us out into the kitchen. There were little cakes she had made, spread out on the table. Each of us was allowed to have one. The cakes tasted strange and dry; they were not sweet. Aunt Hanna told us this was because she couldn't get the proper ingredients.

After we ate our dessert, it was time to go home. Walking back to our apartment, Papa was still in a bad mood. Maman said she wished he had not become so angry in front of the new family. They, too, had their troubles.

"But I don't believe these people!" cried Papa. "They're kidding themselves! They don't have the slightest idea how bad things will be for us if we do get caught! They just can't see the truth of what's happening all around us."

We were crossing the bridge and Papa made no attempt to keep me from hearing what he had to say. It was as if he wanted me to understand just how much danger we were in, despite the fact that I was still a small child. I had the idea, that night, that the police were hiding behind every tree and building, or watching us from way up in the hills. I wondered why we stayed if even the French people were bad. "Should we go somewhere else?"

Maman laughed at my question. "There is nowhere else to go, *mon petit lapin* [my little rabbit]," she said. "Almost the entire world is at war."

The Town Crier

In November 1942, the Fedous were asked to hide a radio in their upstairs apartment. The radio was specially designed to receive broadcasts from the BBC in London. At intervals, cryptic messages were transmitted to Resistance fighters from the Free French forces in Britain.

One day there was a shattering broadcast from Nazi-controlled Radio-Paris. Due to the recent British-American landing on the North African coast, the Germans would soon cross the demarcation line into the unoccupied zone, supposedly to prevent another Allied landing along the Mediterranean coast. Even Marshal Pétain protested the invasion; it was in direct violation of the terms of the armistice. Now we were in more danger than ever before. Soon the Germans would advance into the Vichy zone, and we would have to live in fear of them as well as of the French police. It was just a matter of time before the Gestapo arrived.

I listened to Papa and Maman as they debated over what to do. I would return from school, and they would be discussing the same subject: "Should we go to Marseille? To Nice?"

Papa finally decided against any move. "Those are big cities," he said to Maman. "Even though the Italians are supposedly protecting Jews in Nice, the Nazis are sure to get wind of it. Besides, if the Nazis are moving into the unoccupied zone, perhaps they will take over the coastal cities as well. But here, why would they want to set up headquarters in a tiny village? That would be a waste of manpower. And we have people here who are willing to protect us. Perhaps the Nazis will leave St. Juéry and Arthès in the hands of the French police. After all, the Germans have a war to fight."

So we did not leave. But we faced other problems simply because we were in hiding in a small town. Eventually, people found out "who was where" and what was going on. There were those who made it their business to denounce Jews to the French police.

In St. Juéry and Arthès, news came to us through a town crier. He was French and lived in our village. I was enthralled by his navy blue uniform with its red and gold trim, and the *képi*, or cap, he wore on his head. He looked like one of Uncle Heinrich's old soldier dolls that he kept on a high shelf in the armoire. The town crier carried a drum, which he would beat at precisely the same hour each evening as he marched up and down the streets, proclaiming the news in a booming voice—war news in particular. We rarely paid attention to his reports; we knew the "news" was distorted at best; at worst, it was simply falsified information designed to throw members of the Resistance off the trail of the Nazi supply trucks that gradually began to pass through the surrounding countryside.

I knew what the town crier looked like; I had seen him often enough. When I noticed him walking up our street one afternoon, dressed in simple, civilian clothes, I believed he must be on his way home, or perhaps running an errand. I went upstairs to our apartment and opened the door. Maman was there, sitting by the window, sewing. She asked me about my day at school. Just as I finished telling her, there was a knock at the door. Maman froze, holding up her hand to silence me. She knew Papa was not due home for another hour, and the Fedous had gone into Albi.

When Maman went to the door and opened it, I recognized the town crier standing there.

"What do you want?" Maman asked in a stern voice.

"I believe we have some business to discuss, Madame," he responded.

Maman did not understand. She allowed the man to come into the room and closed the door behind him.

"What is it you want?" she asked again, in French.

I walked over and stood behind Maman, looking up into the man's wide face. His hair was thin and graying. He spoke in a low voice, as though fearful of being overheard.

"Madame, I realize you are fairly new to the village, but surely you are aware by now of the situation here. A man in my line of work can hardly turn a deaf ear to certain conversations. I know where the Jews are hidden in Arthès, and I know that you, yourself, are Jewish. Unless you can persuade me otherwise, I am afraid I will have to report your husband's whereabouts to the police."

"I have no husband," Maman retorted quickly. "He was killed in Morocco. He fought in the Legion."

"That's a lie, Madame," the man said with a patient smile. "I saw him leave for the factory this morning. In fact, I followed him all the way to the Sauts du Tarn."

Maman's eyes widened. I held on to her hand. I did not know whether to run and warn Papa not to come home or to stay with Maman in case something happened to her. But instinctively, Maman knew how to deal with the man. She walked over to the armoire, and, standing at the door, I saw her take out her purse.

"How much do you want?" she asked.

"All of it. Everything that's in the purse."

Maman turned the money over to the man without

another word. He counted it and smiled. "Good. Well done. That should keep your husband safe for the time being."

"For the time being? And how long is that?"

At the door, the man turned and smiled. "As I said, Madame, for the present, your husband will not be reported."

As soon as Papa heard the story that afternoon, he became enraged. "That someone would have the gall to blackmail us on top of everything else! We hardly have enough money for food as it is! But why am I surprised? Things will no doubt get worse the longer the war goes on."

"Do you think he will be back?" Maman asked hesitantly.

"Of course he'll be back! He's got a profitable business going now. The Jews in this village are at his mercy. There's nothing we can do but continue to pay him off. Fortunately, he didn't get the money you keep in the box."

"But, Benno," Maman protested, "how can we afford to pay him off again? We need the money."

"Do you want to get arrested?"

"Of course not, but we could leave, after all. We could go into the mountains and hide for a while. Then he will think we've left Arthès for good."

Papa shook his head. He was angry and tired of moving. Now that the Nazis were taking over the Vichy zone, no place was safe. With a young child to care for, he believed that a small village was preferable to the mountains or a large city.

There was nothing my parents could do but pay off the town crier whenever he demanded it. Uncle Oscar and Joseph Kahn soon faced the same dilemma. They, too, were forced to pay the man off in order to remain in the village with their families. It was better, they said, to keep a known denouncer quiet than to be caught in a roundup. And the roundups were occurring with more frequency all around us.

Papa paid the town crier out of what he made at the factory, which left very little money for my parents to live on. As the town crier continued to demand more and more,

Maman was forced to sell the few treasured possessions she still had in our apartment. She was terrified that we would run out of money and the man would turn Papa in.

As the winter came, I continued to attend the *école communale*, the village school, but was told to come straight home every afternoon. I was not allowed to linger in the schoolyard with other children. There were pickups for the farm children who came into Arthès to go to school, but those of us who lived in the village had to walk home. Maman made sure that she was always home in the afternoons to meet me. She had anticipated that, with the arrival of the Nazis, women and children would be in far more danger than before.

Some mornings, my parents kept me home from school, and Papa did not go to the factory. We were always on edge, never knowing when the Germans would actually arrive in our small, secluded village. The supervisor at the Sauts du Tarn complex gave warning to the Jewish men who worked for him whenever he suspected there would be a roundup or an inspection of the factory. On those days my father did not go to work, and a Madame Sachs, from the village, came to help me with my lessons. She, too, was a refugee. In return for her tutoring services, Maman gave her food or invited her to stay with us for lunch.

I was five years old and always bored with my lessons, for I had so little playtime. I squirmed in my chair as Madame Sachs went over the mistakes in my lessons with me. I wanted to be outside, playing with my friends; but they, too, were shut inside. At least in school we had recreation periods when we would go out and play in the schoolyard, but whenever I was at home, Maman kept me inside. I could never play in the street. The moment Madame Sachs left for the day, Maman would occupy me in all sorts of ways in order to turn my attention from the outdoors.

One afternoon, when Maman was not looking and Papa had not yet come home for his lunch, I slipped out of the apartment and went out to the street to play. I had my doll with me, and several pieces of bread, which seemed enough for me to survive an afternoon away from Maman. I was determined that she would not find me because I knew, the moment she did, I would be punished and never permitted to go outside alone again.

It was a blustery afternoon. The sky was more gray than blue, and the wind turned my ears red. I remember the tree branches swaying in the gales. They seemed to urge me forward: "Hurry up, little one! This way!" I found myself walking farther and farther away from the apartment—which Maman had strictly forbidden. She had told me on numerous occasions never to leave our street without her. I walked up the steep incline to the corner. Far in the distance, I could see the hills rising up over the red-tiled rooftops of Arthès. I wanted to be there, up in the hills, where I could look down over everything.

As I walked, I sang to myself and dreamed up stories about the Germans and the French police. Perhaps they would begin a war among themselves and forget about the Jews.

I was about two blocks from our building when I noticed a narrow door that was slightly ajar. I stopped in front of the door and saw a woman standing there by the window, kneading dough. I could smell bread baking. Warm air issued from the kitchen out into the cool afternoon. On the windowsill was a wooden bowl filled with potatoes, and there were many apples lined up on the table. I knew what apples were, and I wanted one. The year before, I had watched Maman drying apples on a string. We had eaten them all winter. Maybe if I stood there long enough, the woman would notice me.

"*Bonjour, Mademoiselle,*" she said at last. "It gets so hot in here when I am baking. That's why I leave the door open a crack, but with the wind, it blows wide open." She was smiling. "Do you want to come in?" She was a short woman with a kind face, but her gray hair, pulled back into a bun, made her look somewhat severe. She had a friendly, soft voice.

I stepped just inside the doorway. "*Bonjour, Madame,*" I replied. I did not know what to say next. Should I ask the woman for a potato or an apple? "*Comment t'appelles-tu?*" she asked me, wanting to know my name.

"*Je m'appelle Renée.*"

"*Quel age as-tu?*"

I told her I was five years old. The woman smiled and continued kneading the dough, first into a big ball, and then into long strips.

"*J'ai faim, Madame,*" I finally confessed, holding my stomach to let her know how hungry I was.

The woman looked up and laughed. She came to the doorway and asked me what I would like to eat. I pointed to the apples.

"Open your apron," she told me. She gathered several potatoes, two or three apples, and some walnuts and put them into my apron. Then she broke a loaf of bread in half and gave me part of it. She told me I would have to walk very slowly back down the street, so as not to drop anything. There were other foods on her shelves that I did not recognize and had never seen before. My apron was getting full, but I knew there was something missing.

"And my father likes wine!" I blurted.

"*Ah, oui!*" The woman laughed. She left the kitchen and returned a moment later with a bottle of wine. I thought she must be a queen, or someone very rich, to have so much good food. I did not realize that she had given me almost all the food she had planned to serve her husband for dinner that night.

"*Merci beaucoup, Madame,*" I said. Then I held up my doll. "Here is my little friend, Jeanine," I offered. "She is for you."

The woman laughed again. It was obvious I could not carry my doll along with the bottle of wine and all the food in my apron, but she would not take my doll from me.

"*Ah, non, Mademoiselle,*" she protested. She placed the doll in my apron so that it covered all the food. "Now no one will be able to see what you have. Hurry home with it, and don't drop anything!"

I thanked her once more, then I was on my way home with enough food to last us a week. Maman would be so proud of me, and Papa would be happy, too, now that he had some wine again. I walked very slowly, carefully placing one foot in front of the other, so that I would not drop any of my precious booty. Somehow I found my way back to our street. I was coming down the steep hill when Maman caught sight of me. She was standing there at the foot of the hill, looking up and down. I wanted to run to her, to hold up the bottle of wine and shout, "Look, Maman!" but I remembered what the lady had said. No one must see what I was carrying in my apron until I got it safely home.

I reached our door. Maman looked very angry. "Where have you been, Renée? Why didn't you come when I called you?"

I swallowed. "I went to get some food for us, Maman."

"What?"

As I started to explain, Maman opened the door to our apartment building and marched me up the stairs. Papa was waiting there, a worried expression on his face. I opened out my apron, and Maman picked up my doll. Then she gasped, horrified.

"No!" she cried. "Benno, look!"

Papa did not know what to say. He put the bottle of wine on the table and unloaded the rest of the food.

"Where did you get this, Renée?" Maman demanded.

"From the lady up the street. She lives near us. She is very nice, and she gave it to me."

"She gave it to you? Are you sure you didn't take this food, Renée?"

"I am sure, Maman. I told her I was hungry, and she opened out my apron and put all this food into it."

"What is her name?"

"I don't know, Maman."

Maman looked at Papa and said, "We have to take it back."

Papa nodded.

Then I began to cry. "But she gave it to me. It was a present! She told me to take it home and not to let anyone take it from me!" I reached for an apple, but Maman would not let me have it. She did not believe my story. Already, she was putting the food into the bag she carried with her whenever she went to the market.

"Come along, Renée," she said, taking my hand firmly in her own. "We are going to take this food right back. I want you to show me where this woman lives."

Maman and I walked down the stairs in silence. I pointed up the street, and Maman took my hand firmly and led me up the hill. When we reached the corner, we turned right. "Now, where is it?" she asked.

I pointed up ahead to the second street on the right. Maman led me along the walk, we turned the corner, and then we were on the woman's street. I saw the window, but it was not open. The door, too, had been closed. I pointed to the house. Maman stopped in the street. "This is it?"

"Yes, Maman."

Maman knocked on the door. In a few minutes, we heard footsteps and then the door opened. The same woman answered.

"Ah," she said, "*bonjour, Renée.*"

Maman quickly held out the bag of food. "I am afraid that my daughter took this food from you earlier this afternoon, Madame. I am very sorry. Please accept our apology."

"But, Madame," said the woman, "I gave your daughter the food. She seemed to be hungry. She did not steal it."

"Even so," Maman went on, "we cannot take it. That would be unfair to you. Thank you for your kindness." She turned as if to go.

The woman looked down at me, smiling, and offered me an apple. Then she insisted that Maman keep the food and the wine. I looked up at Maman, who laughed and said I could keep the apple.

"You have a lovely little girl," the woman said. "I hope you'll come to visit me again, Renée."

Maman thanked the woman. "She is difficult to keep track of at times!" she said. Then Maman introduced herself.

The woman told us her name was Madame Valat. "Please feel free to visit us again. My husband and I, we have a radio. Perhaps you would like to come and listen some evening. You would certainly be most welcome. We do not have many visitors in the winter."

Maman was surprised that the Valats had a radio. She nodded, smiling. "You are very kind, Madame," she said to the woman. It was not until later, as she recounted the story to Papa, that Maman began to suspect that the Valats were members of the Resistance group.

We thanked Madame Valat again, and Maman and I ate apples on our way home. "I'm sorry I did not believe you," Maman said to me, "but you must never again leave the apartment without me. Do you hear me?"

"Yes, Maman." At least I had not been forbidden to go out into the street ever again. I asked Maman if we could go over to visit Madame Valat next week.

"Perhaps, Renée," she said. "She seemed to be a nice woman. But you mustn't ever ask people for food. It is very rude, do you understand?"

"Yes, Maman."

The next morning, Maman asked Madame Fedou about the Valats. As it happened, Madame Fedou knew the woman and said that she could definitely be trusted not to give us away. The Valats had a daughter who was about the age of Lucette Fedou, and the two girls knew each other. So began another friendship in the village. Perhaps we began to feel a little more secure. The longer we stayed in Arthès, the more people we met, people who were charitable, kind, and trustworthy. These were people who were willing to risk their own lives and safety for us. And they became our friends.

In the Valats' Cellar

As the weeks wore on, Maman and Papa were worried by the ever-increasing number of roundups occurring in Albi. We often had to run into the fields and hide for several hours, having heard reports of roundups in the neighboring towns. Sometimes we met other Jews there who had come from Albi; they had been fortunate enough to escape their places of hiding before the French police came for them.

During this time, rumors began to circulate that the French police were redoubling their efforts to track down the Jews still in hiding in the small villages. The police had to fill their quotas in order to placate the Nazis, who had strict timetables and refused to send trains to the east unless they were filled to capacity. We did not know whether to believe the rumors or not, but Maman grew more and more hesitant about leaving the apartment. The Protestant minister who had taken Papa to Toulouse in August got in touch with him through an intermediary. This messenger warned Papa that things were getting worse, not better—particularly for the foreign and "stateless" Jews, very few of whom, he was told, were left in France.

The rumors my parents had heard were true, and Papa was urged to stop working at the Sauts du Tarn factory altogether and to stay inside at all times.

"If we do that," Papa cried, "we will have no money to pay off the town crier!"

The minister's friend told Papa that he would try to arrange something. He urged Papa to continue following all of Monsieur Fedou's instructions. "If you hear there is going to be a roundup, or if you see anything suspicious yourself, get out of here. Go into the fields, climb into the hills, just get out. The first place they will look for you, Monsieur Caper, is here, in your own apartment, or at the factory."

"I understand," Papa said. "You don't have to tell me!"

He and Maman told the intermediary to thank the minister for his concern, and the man promised to stay in touch with Maman. Papa was smiling after the man left; he could not understand why the Protestant minister had taken such an interest in our welfare, enough to send an emissary to warn us. The minister seemed as determined as the Fedous to protect us.

I attended school intermittently, but for several weeks Papa did not go to work at the factory at all. He may have been tired of living clandestinely, but he knew what the penalty would be for taking risks. The minister's words of caution had their intended effect on Papa.

Each morning that I went to school, I would sit in the one-room schoolhouse, only half-listening to the lessons, wondering whether my parents would still be there when I returned home. There were perhaps forty students at the village school, ten in each row of desks. The desks were arranged evenly on both sides, with an aisle in the middle. At the front of the room was a platform on which the teacher's desk and chair stood. I can still see the wrought-iron gate in front of the school, and the steps leading up to the building. In the mornings, even in the winter, we would all linger on the steps, not wanting to go inside and begin the lessons for the day.

I was always one of the first to finish my lessons in the afternoon and would turn to my closest neighbor. Invariably, I would be spotted by the school mistress and forced to go to the board and conjugate verbs, or go to the back of the room to complete yet another section in my lesson book. With very little effort, I'd finish my work in the allotted time, and then sit by the doorway, bored and tired, waiting to go home. In the back of my mind was the persistent worry, "What if Papa and Maman are not there when I get back?"

One windy January afternoon, I started home from school alone. As I was walking, I noticed that there was no one else out on the street. Usually, I would see one or two men coming out of the *tabac*, or a woman taking down her laundry from a clothesline, but that afternoon, I saw no one at all. "Perhaps it is because of the cold," I thought.

When I reached the side stairs leading to our apartment, I saw Andrée Fedou sitting on the bottom step. Her arms were crossed in front of her, her hands tucked under her arms for warmth, since she had no gloves. The minute she saw me, she stood up and said, "Let's go for a walk, Renée." She took my hand.

"But I have to see my parents," I insisted. "I have to put my books away."

"I know," she nodded, "but you'll be able to do that in a little while. Just come with me."

Andrée led me up the street. We were walking fast against the bitter wind. Still I saw no one and asked Andrée why there was nobody around. "I'll tell you in a little while," she answered.

We walked to the corner and then turned right. As we started up the next street, I began to recognize houses and thought we must be on our way to the Valats' house. I did not know anyone else who lived along those streets.

When we turned down the next street, I recognized the front of Madame Valat's house. The door was closed and all the curtains were drawn at the windows. There was no smell of baking bread that day, only the cold wind. Andrée led me up the walk to the door and knocked. In a moment, a tall, gray-haired man opened it and told us to come in. Bending down, he shook my hand and said, "You must be Renée. I am Monsieur Valat."

"*Bonjour, Monsieur,*" I said.

Andrée and I were led down a flight of steps into a cellar room. In the room, I saw many people: Maman and Papa, Monsieur and Madame Fedou, their daughter Lucette, and Madame Valat, who was slicing potato skins into a bowl. There were several men whom I had never seen before. They were standing against the grimy plaster wall. Maman motioned to me to come and sit beside her on a long, overturned crate. No one was talking.

"What's wrong, Maman?" I whispered.

Maman explained that there had been several raids on houses the night before, and many of the Jewish families who had recently come to the village had been taken away.

"Why weren't we taken, Maman?"

"Because we are fortunate enough to have a place to stay, and the Fedous are looking after us," she answered simply.

I heard someone say to Papa, "We think it was the town crier who reported the new families to the police. Several men who were working for the Resistance were also taken, and Monsieur Valat thinks the town crier is the one who denounced them. I guess he didn't give us away this time because we have thus far been able to pay him off."

A man in the corner soon began to adjust the knob of a radio. Monsieur Valat told the man to hurry, that the broadcast was scheduled to begin at any moment. Maman told me that everyone was waiting to hear a broadcast from Radio-Paris. In seconds, we heard static, and then a voice speaking in chopped phrases. Papa said, "Keep the volume down," despite the fact that we had difficulty trying to hear. We all listened to the deep voice that filled the room.

The announcer reported that a new law had gone into

effect establishing a new police force, which was to be called La Milice Française. The saboteurs would be the particular target of the Milice, as well as those members of the underground who sought to avoid deportation to the forced labor camps in Germany. The official decree had been signed into law several hours earlier, the radio announcer said.

When the radio address came to an end, there was an awkward silence in the room. The men who had been leaning against the plaster wall were no longer there. One of them was called Michel; he was Lucette Fedou's fiancé. Maman took my hand, and we followed Andrée up the rickety steps to the Valats' kitchen. Lucette was standing there: she had come up to find out where the men had gone.

"Where is Michel?" Andrée asked.

"He went outside with the others. They went to smoke a cigarette and get some air."

Andrée nodded.

"This is bad for the Resistance," Lucette murmured to her sister. "With this new police force, it will be easier for Papa to get caught."

Andrée did not say anything. I understood only much later that Monsieur Fedou must be involved in fighting the Nazis as a member of an underground Resistance group. In a moment, Madame Valat came up the stairs, followed by Madame Fedou. Together they had made a pot of soup and now began ladling it into bowls to serve to everyone. Madame Valat told Andrée to go outside and call the men back in. When the men returned to the kitchen, their faces were somber; some of them were obviously angry.

Michel turned to Lucette and said in a low voice, "We're going to join the Resistance."

"*Oh, mon Dieu, mon Dieu!*" cried Madame Fedou, who had overheard what he had said. She simultaneously dropped the ladle in the soup pot and turned to look at Michel as though he were crazy.

"Didn't you hear the radio announcement?" Lucette cried, visibly upset. "You fools, you'll get caught before the week is over! It's bad enough that Papa is in even more danger. You'll just make things worse for us in the village. You'll attract the police, rather than keep them away."

"And what about all the people who were taken away last night?" Michel asked. "Who is going to replace them in the underground?"

"It's not up to you to pick up where they left off!"

"Somebody has to take the responsibility," another man said. "Are we just going to give up at the slightest sign of intimidation by that old Pétain, sitting in the Hôtel du Parc in Vichy? Anyway, he's too old to know what he's just done to us!"

Madame Valat made no comment. She remained composed and continued ladling soup into bowls. The men sat down casually at the kitchen table and ate their soup, gratefully, in silence. They had made up their minds. Lucette was still standing in the corner of the room, glaring at Michel.

When we returned to the cellar to rejoin Papa, Monsieur Valat, and Monsieur Fedou, Maman said, "Those men are going to join the Resistance! Lucette is terribly upset."

"*Non!* Really?" Papa asked. He turned to Monsieur Valat. "Are they crazy? Do they want to get themselves killed? Or sent to Germany, to a work camp?"

"Surely they listened to the announcement?" Maman said. "Surely they understood—?"

Monsieur Valat gave a laugh. "It's because of the announcement," he explained. "They feel it is their duty. To them, the Vichy government has betrayed us. Those officials have been playing a game with the Germans and have ended by handing everything over to them on a silver platter. Besides," he added, "we can at least do our best to protect the people God has put into our care."

Papa looked down gratefully.

After several hours, the Valats' house gradually emptied out.

The men left first; Lucette and Andrée watched them start out into the night and fade into the shadows. Maman and I followed Madame Fedou and her daughters home. Papa followed us several minutes later. Our departures were staggered so that we would not draw attention to the Valats' house.

When we returned to our own apartment, there was no trace of a forced entry by the police; no one had come looking for us while we had been gone. We had heard no news from St. Juéry that day, but it was too dangerous for Papa to make a trip to check on Uncle Oscar's family. We hoped that they, too, were safe.

The Fedous and the Valats got together and developed a plan. Whenever there was real trouble in the village, the Valats would hide us in their coal cellar. I was instructed that if I happened to come home from school and find an empty apartment, I was never to go immediately to the Valats' house; that would give our hiding place away, if we were, in fact, being watched. I was to go to the Fedous' and wait there until Andrée told me it was safe to go to the Valats' house. Fortunately, Maman and Papa were usually at home, waiting to greet me.

On one occasion that winter, we had to spend two nights in the Valats' cellar. We slept among the sacks of potatoes and the coal. Madame Valat would bring food down to us, and we were able to move about, but we could not leave the house. The first night we were there was a Friday. I was surprised when Papa said that we were going to observe the Sabbath. "We owe God our gratitude for bringing us here," he said. I remember how he spoke the kiddush, the prayer over the wine, in a very low voice, so that the Valats could not hear; and the next night, the havdalah, the prayer marking the end of the Sabbath, and hoping for a good week. I was enthralled; I had never observed the Sabbath rituals before but somehow felt comforted by the prayers.

When Sunday morning came, Madame Valat, who was a

Catholic, came down the steps to ask Maman if she would like to accompany her to church.

"If the people from the village see you in the church, they will assume you are a Catholic, and not a woman in hiding," Madame Valat explained. "You could be visiting a relative, or perhaps you've come to the south of France to look for work in the fields, but they won't jump to the conclusion that you are Jewish if you're standing in the Catholic church. It might be a good way to protect yourself and your family. There are other Jews in the village who are going."

"Really? But won't it be too dangerous? I won't know what to do. I won't know any prayers."

"Just imitate whatever I do," she suggested.

"But if the town crier already knows we are Jewish," Papa interrupted, "what's the point?"

"You never know when some woman from the village might spot Madame Caper. Later, that same woman might be taken off and interrogated by the police concerning Jews in the village. If she is under the impression that your wife is a Catholic, and perhaps saw her walking to the church one morning with me, it would not cross her mind to mention Madame Caper to the police."

So Maman put on her best dress and went upstairs to join Madame Valat and Madame Fedou, who had walked over to the house to accompany Madame Valat to mass.

Papa and I stayed down in the cellar and heard Maman and the women leave. Papa was very quiet; I could tell that he was worried that something might happen to Maman while she was out in the open.

After some time had passed, there were footsteps above us, and Monsieur Valat came halfway down the stairs.

"Everything all right, Monsieur?" he called to Papa.

"Oh, yes, my friend. You did not go to the church with your wife?" Papa asked.

"No. Not today. I like to keep my wife on her toes. Now

she will have to pray twice as hard for me!" he said with a throaty laugh. "You know how these women are, always going to church. The bad thing is, the priest knows me, and you can be sure, before the day is out, he'll be at the door, wondering why I wasn't at mass!" After a moment, he said, "Come on up here, Monsieur. I want to show you something."

"All right," Papa called. "Be right up."

I followed Papa up the stairs to the bright kitchen. Our eyes were unaccustomed to the light, and we had to squint to see because of the glare. Monsieur Valat led us into a tiny room off the kitchen, which we had never seen before. Monsieur Fedou was already seated there at the narrow table, shuffling a deck of cards. He greeted us as we walked in.

Monsieur Valat turned to Papa and said in a very low tone, "I do not like to leave you alone here in the house, Monsieur Caper, but if ever you are in the house by yourself and I am not close by, if you hear anything suspicious, come into this room at once. Don't go down into the cellar because you won't have time. When this door is bolted from the inside, it appears to be part of the wall from the outside."

He demonstrated how this was so by taking Papa back into the kitchen and calling to me to lock the door from the inside.

I did what Monsieur Valat told me, and I heard Papa say, "Amazing! I never noticed that before."

I opened the door, and the men came back into the room. "Few people ever do," Monsieur Valat went on. "When there are many of you, we have to put you down in the cellar because there is just not enough room in here to hide everyone. But when it's just you, be sure to come in here. You can be certain that if there is ever a raid, the police will always look in the cellar."

The three men sat down at the table to play cards. Papa told me to sit quietly and work on my lessons, but for a long time, I played with Madame Valat's gray cat and listened to the conversation Papa was having with the two men. It might have been any normal Sunday morning when three friends gathered to play cards and talk, were it not for the fact that we were Jewish and in hiding. We always had to be on the alert. Surrounding us in the small room were shelves of books. Monsieur Valat was very interested in history and read all the time. I used to wish that he would read to me as Uncle Heinrich had done, but he never suggested it, and I was too shy to ask him. Papa said that he was a very knowledgeable man; he knew his history better than anyone in the village. Monsieur Valat offered to let Papa borrow his books. "But don't take too many off the shelves at one time." He laughed. "The books also help to soundproof the room!"

That morning, Papa and Monsieur Valat were talking about what became of the Jewish people when they were arrested. I pretended to be absorbed in my lessons, and Papa seemed to forget that I was there, listening to everything they said.

"It's worse for the families who have just arrived," Monsieur Fedou explained. "Before anyone has a chance to get to know them, to find a place for them, they're taken off in a roundup. Already, I have three families outside the village, hiding in an old barn, waiting for a place to stay."

"Can you imagine how it is in the occupied zone?" Papa asked quietly. "There, they are at the mercy of the Gestapo."

"You forget," Monsieur Valat corrected, "that now, all of France is the occupied zone. Soon, the Gestapo will be here as well."

"You think so?"

"I'm afraid so. They're already in Albi, from what I've heard."

Monsieur Fedou looked up, suddenly remembering that I was in the room and could easily be frightened by their talk. He changed the subject slightly. He turned to Papa and asked, "This anti-Semitism, Benno. What is it? What does it actually mean?"

Papa slapped down a card on the table and sat for a moment, dumbstruck. "You mean that, with all that has happened, and is still happening, you don't know what it means?"

"You don't understand, old friend," Monsieur Valat tried to

explain. "The Jewish people have lived in this area since the Middle Ages when they came from Spain, during the Inquisition. We have coexisted peacefully. What we don't understand is how all this came about. What have the Germans got against the Jews? What have the French got against the Jews?"

Papa put his hand of cards facedown on the table and smiled. "That's a long history lesson," he said. "It may be true that for years France has been a haven for our people, but it wasn't always that way and it's quite different elsewhere. In Germany, the Nazis have developed the insane myth that the Jews are plotting to take over the world. They have perpetuated this propaganda and brainwashed the German population so thoroughly that we are considered a blight on the earth. They want to destroy our entire race, as if we were less than animals! And, make no mistake, there are people here in France, as well as in other countries, who will help the Nazis carry out their diabolical program. Look at all these people who are so eager to denounce us. We're a threat, you see—a threat to the country's economy, because they think we'll take all the jobs; a threat to the country's culture, which they think we'll destroy, or somehow 'dilute'; and we're a threat to the country's security. They want to blame the fact that France is at war with Germany on us! Look at the Milice, a police force made up of supposedly enlightened Frenchmen like yourselves!"

"But why, Papa?"

The three men turned around, suddenly conscious of my having overheard Papa's words.

"I have asked myself many times, Renée," Papa said simply, "but I can't tell you. I don't understand it. This is not the first time in history that the Jews have been treated this way. I only know that there is nothing we can do now."

The men continued playing cards but said no more on the subject. I still was not quite sure I understood what anti-Semitism meant, or why it existed. I was surprised that Monsieur Fedou had asked Papa. It was as if he had not fully understood what he was fighting for until that moment.

After a while, Maman and Madame Valat returned to the house. They were surprised to find us upstairs, and Maman asked me what I had done all morning and whether I had finished my lessons. We all gathered in the kitchen, and Madame Valat began to prepare a late breakfast for us.

Within minutes, there was a knock at the door, and Madame Fedou soon entered the room with a tall man whom they called Monsieur le Curé. I laughed to myself when I saw him, because he was dressed in what appeared to be a long black dress. Maman explained to me that this man was the priest of the village, and his garment was called a *soutane*.

"Ah! What did I tell you! What did I tell you!" Monsieur Valat cried to Papa, as he pulled out his watch chain and checked his pocket watch. "Not an hour has passed since mass is over and here is Monsieur le Curé come to take me to task! Come in, come in, my friend," he said, greeting the priest.

"You're right, old man." The priest laughed, running a hand through his graying hair. "I couldn't let a week go by without seeing your weather-beaten face. And as it happens, I have some news for you."

"I hoped you might. Come in here."

Before Monsieur Valat ushered the priest into the hidden room, Madame Fedou introduced us to him. He had already met Maman, but he shook my hand and called me *un petit ange*, a little angel. He had kind, deep blue eyes and a laugh that made you want to laugh, too. He shook Papa's hand cordially and then followed Monsieur Valat and Monsieur Fedou into the hidden room.

"Those men, they're crazy when they get together." Madame Valat smiled, shaking her head. She was stirring some kind of batter in a deep bowl.

Maman began to set the table. "Will the priest be staying to eat with us?" she asked.

"*Ah, non,*" Madame Fedou whispered. We laughed at her,

because she was trying to listen at the door of the hidden room. "He has many families to visit today."

Maman nodded and placed woven napkins at each end of the table. We went over my lessons as the two women finished preparing the meal. Lucette and Michel were in and out that afternoon, hoping to talk with the priest about their wedding, but Madame Valat finally convinced them to wait until another time when he was not so busy.

Monsieur Valat and Monsieur Fedou talked with the priest for a long time. While they were still in the hidden room, there was another knock at the door, and this time, Papa's friend, the minister, asked to see Monsieur Valat. "You come, too," the minister told Papa. "This concerns you."

With that, Papa and the minister also entered the hidden room and joined the other men. When they finally emerged, and the priest took his leave of us, little was said. We knew that serious matters had been discussed, but I did not realize, until many years had passed, that much of what had been planned in that little room off the kitchen that morning would affect my entire childhood.

Once we had eaten, Madame Fedou returned to our apartment and sent word to us by way of Andrée that it was safe for us to go home. We thanked the Valats for their protection and their kindness to us and were soon out in the street, walking back to our building. Papa was to follow later that evening, when it was dark, accompanied by Monsieur Fedou.

As Maman and I walked, I asked her what it had been like to go to mass.

"It was hard to understand," she told me. "I just sat there and watched. They have a lot of singing, but it's in a different language. I know there were many women from the village there who saw me. I tried to imitate what Madame Valat and Madame Fedou did when I could. Maybe now the people will think we are Catholics, and we will be left alone."

Interrogation

I come home from school to find my mother gone. It is the sixteenth of November, 1943, Maman's birthday. Madame Sachs, from the village, is sitting at the table when I come in the door.

"Where is Maman?" I feel the knot of fear tighten in my stomach.

"Don't worry," Madame Sachs tells me. "She's gone to visit your cousin, Evelyne. She'll be back soon."

I know that Evelyne has just had an operation. She had to have her tonsils out. Maman must have gone over to help Aunt Hanna. I find a piece of candy my mother has left for me on the table. I know then that everything is all right. The candy is Maman's special signal to me that she will be back as soon as she can.

I take off my sweater and begin to unlace the shoes that have become so small for me that I now have blisters on the sides of my feet. My shoe is cracked on one side, and water seeps in whenever I step in a puddle.

I know Maman cannot find a pair of shoes for me anywhere in the village, and so I do not complain. Everyone else has the same problem, especially the children. Leather is so scarce that our shoes have to be resoled with wood.

Madame Sachs begins to fold bits of paper over and over into small animals or objects. Watching her closely, I try to mimic what she is doing. She is very clever with her hands, and in no time we have made a sailboat and a swan, two presents I will save to give to Maman tonight.

After we have put the presents away in the drawer, I take out my lesson books, and Madame Sachs begins to go over my lessons with me. Sitting at the table in the oppressive quiet of afternoon in the village, we are entirely unprepared for the sudden sound of loud, heavy boots on the stairs. Madame Sachs jumps up. I do not move. "Hide! Hide!" she whispers, but I do not have enough time. There is nowhere in the small room to lose myself.

There are several loud raps on the door.

"*Attendez!*[Wait!]" Madame Sachs calls. She tells me not to say anything, no matter who it is. Then she unbolts the door.

Two men enter the room. One is tall and has a mustache; the other is short. They wear black jackets, khaki-colored shirts, blue pants, black bérets, and the wide black leather belts Aunt Sophie had described to Papa when she told him about the police coming to look for Uncle Heinrich. I know at once that these men are the enemy. They must be les Miliciens, members of the new French police force.

One of the men pushes Madame Sachs aside. They know right away that she is not my mother. While the tall man comes toward me, the other one searches the room, peering into the small closet that doubles as our kitchen area.

"What do you want with her?" Madame Sachs demands.

"We want to question her," the tall man says.

"Can't you see that she's only a little girl? She doesn't know anything."

"Shut up!" says the short man. "We're not here to talk to you. We want to talk to her."

Both men grab me by the arms. I remain quite still, hardly raising my head.

"Little girl," says the tall man, "where is your father?"

"I haven't seen him in a thousand years," I say.

My parents trained me long ago; I know never to disclose their whereabouts to anyone, least of all to someone in a uniform. I know how to lie in order to protect myself, so I exaggerate the lie, thinking that if I say "a thousand years," they will certainly believe me.

"Well, the last time you saw him, which way did he go?"

I make up a direction and point. "But it's so long ago, you'll never find him."

"It's true," Madame Sachs intervenes.

"Shut up!" the short man says to her, and then to me: "You're lying." He is speaking in a cool, low tone. "Look, we know who you are. We know all about you, your name, your *real* name. You are Jewish, aren't you?"

I shake my head vehemently.

I am not sure, afterward, whether they have actually found out my true name or if they are trying to trap me. They address me neither as Ruth nor as Renée.

The taller man attempts a gentler approach. "Try to remember. In which direction did Papa go when he left the house this morning?"

I shrug. They know I am lying. My whole body is trembling by this time, and my knees feel weak. I know that at any moment, my father's shift will end and he will be on his way home. I say, "*Je ne sais pas* [I don't know]," in the best southern dialect I can muster. I have picked up this regional accent from my friends at the *école communale* and now am able to mimic it exactly. I want the two policemen to think that I am a native of the region and that they have made a terrible mistake. But what if they have checked my records? What if they have discovered, somehow, that we all hold fake identity cards?

Finally, with two hands, I point in two directions at once.

"Very clever little girl," the short one says to the other. I can tell he will not tolerate lying, and I am afraid he will hit me. I look up into his face for the first time, and I see that his eyes are narrow brown slits. One of his front teeth is cracked and partially chipped. He pushes me back into the chair and shouts, "Which way? Tell us now, or we go and get your mother!"

Behind them, I can see Madame Sachs shaking her head. Does she think I am stupid? Of course I am not going to give my parents away.

Again, I point in the direction opposite the road that my father always takes to reach the factory at St. Juéry. "I think it was that way," I say, "but I'm not sure. It was a long time ago."

The two men look at each other and then turn to look at Madame Sachs. I am sure they mean to take me away and kill me in Papa's place.

"She is telling the truth," Madame Sachs mutters. "I'm sure if you just follow that road, you'll find the man you are looking for. Now look at the poor thing. You've scared her to death!"

They are staring at me. I burst into tears.

"You'd better be telling the truth, little girl," says the short man, "or we might come back for you."

They go to the door, open it, and walk down the dark stairs. Before they reach the street, I hear the tall man say to the other, "We didn't get a single one today. We're surely going to lose our jobs."

Madame Sachs slams the door after them and hurries to lock it. Then she comes over to hug me. I am sobbing; now that the interrogation is over, I begin to understand Maman's fears and the great danger we are in. But I cannot understand why these people are hounding us. Why do we have to hide while others do not? I understand now why Maman had locked me up in the coal cellar so many times in Toulouse, trying to keep me safe the only way she knew how. I remember the cool darkness of that cellar: the cold, slimy walls, the sudden scurrying noises in the corner. That is what prison must be like.

"You're shaking," Madame Sachs says as she holds me. She does not realize that she, too, is shaking.

"Will they come back to get me? Will they find Papa?"

"Hush, Renée," she says. "Your Maman will be home soon."

Maman returned several hours later. A neighbor had warned her, on her way back from St. Juéry, that two Miliciens had been spotted walking up the stairs to our apartment. Maman had been frantic, wondering how she could get word to Papa before his shift ended and he started walking home. Then, panicky, she realized that the police might already be at the factory.

The neighbor reassured Maman that someone with the underground had been sent to intercept Papa on his way home and warn him. To be safe, however, the woman had urged Maman not to return home herself until dark.

When Maman finally came through the door early that evening, I rushed to her and clung to her neck. She cried as I recounted the events of that afternoon. I remember the way she shook her head and covered her face in a gesture of exhaustion and helplessness. My parents were beginning to feel they were on a treadmill, running and running, hoping to escape danger, yet fearing what new dangers might await them in a new place. Anyone who came by might be someone who would harm them—or someone who could help.

"We are not even safe here, in this little village," Maman said.

"They said they would come back for me if they could not find Papa!"

"No," Maman reassured me. "They won't come for you. Poor child. That such a thing should happen when I'm not home!"

Madame Sachs was looking at us with a grave expression on

her face. "You cannot stay here anymore, Madame. It is much too dangerous now. They will know that you are here, that you are sitting here waiting for Monsieur Caper to come home."

"I know," Maman agreed. "As soon as I talk to Madame Fedou, I will know what to do."

Maman did not give Madame Sachs any indication of where we might hide. While she trusted Madame Sachs, she could never be sure whether or not the woman's friends could be trusted. Now Maman would wonder who it was who had given us away.

Soon, Madame Sachs left, and Maman heated soup for us on the little kerosene stove. Our room was nearly dark, except for a lamp burning on the table. Maman believed that, even with the metal shutters closed across the windows, people were able to tell, through the cracks, when the light was on in our room—which was supposed to be a storage area for the adjoining apartment. We spent over an hour terrified that the police would come back. This time, they might take Maman.

At last, there was a noise on the stairs. We both listened, hardly moving. Suppose the police had stayed behind, had watched Maman come home, and were now waiting in the shadows of the stairwell, just in case Papa tried to return that night?

"Get your coat," Maman whispered.

There were two knocks at the door, a pause, and then a third knock. This was the signal the Fedous always used. Cautiously, Maman opened the door.

Andrée Fedou stood there, leaning against the wall. Her face was completely hidden in the shadows. "Hurry, Madame," she instructed Maman. "I'm to take you up the street. We all heard about what happened this afternoon. It's not safe for you now."

Maman nodded. We knew that "up the street" meant the Valats' house. We tiptoed down the steps. Outside, the streets were completely dark and abandoned. Everyone's windows and shutters were closed, bolted against the brief, soundless activities of the Resistance circuit. We moved through the shadows, climbed the hill, and kept close to the buildings. Madame Valat was already waiting for us as we neared the entrance of her house. "Hurry inside," she whispered at the door.

We said good night to Andrée, who started back to her own apartment.

There was only one light on in the Valats' entire house, in the kitchen. They had prepared a snack for us, which we had to eat quickly before hurrying down to the cellar. Henri Valat was sitting near the table, reading a thick, old book. He must read all the time, I thought, like Uncle Heinrich.

"I'm so sorry about this afternoon," Madame Valat apologized. "What a shock for poor Renée."

She led us down the narrow steps into the cellar. By now, I felt at home there; I was used to the smell, the dust. Madame Valat turned on a lamp for us, and there was a pitcher of water in case we were thirsty during the night.

"Until all this dies down," she told us, "you'll be safest down here. So far, the police have not yet discovered this cellar, nor the hidden room upstairs. The Fedous will be watching for your husband; they will tell him to come directly to the house. It is probably best that you talk only when necessary, and remember—only in low tones."

Maman listened carefully to everything Madame Valat told us, then nodded. We both sat down on sacks of coal and tried to eat the remainder of the bread we had brought downstairs. I could not swallow. I had to force myself to chew little pieces of bread and then drink some water. I thought that every noise signaled trouble for us. We were waiting for the worst to happen.

I look at Maman's face in the dim light. She stares straight ahead, her eyes wide and unblinking. She is memorizing every noise in the night and has barely moved since we came down to the cellar.

When I peer into the dark corners and recesses of the room, I can almost see the faces of the two policemen passing among the shadows. I see the man with the chipped tooth and dark eyes. He is laughing, his face enlarging to impossible proportions. He knows my name; he knows everything about me, especially how I hate the dark.

His figure grows taller and taller until I run under him, run between his shiny, black boots. And then I'm free. I run and run into the fields and along the road, back the way we came. I am running to Toulouse, searching everywhere along the roads for Uncle Heinrich, for Jeannette, for anyone who knows me. The corn and sunflowers in the distance look like hair standing on end. Everywhere, the low hills look like heaps of bodies. I think the bodies belong to the people who have been hunted down and captured by the police. That's what becomes of them.

I turn to look over my shoulder and, to my horror, I see the policeman there on the road. He is running after me, calling my name. I try to run faster, but the ground suddenly opens up under my feet, and I must dodge the big holes. No matter where I run, the earth opens up, wider and wider, and I feel myself falling.

"Renée! Renée!"

Maman was nudging me out of sleep. I sat up on a bag of coal and turned to see Papa coming down the steps.

"Papa!" I shouted as he hurried down to us.

Monsieur and Madame Valat followed behind Papa and sat on the steps, warning us to keep our voices down.

As he took Maman in his arms, Papa said, "Happy Birthday, Lissy." He was smiling. He had outsmarted the police.

Maman laughed and cried at the same time, plucking the bits of dried grass from Papa's sweater. She said that this had been the worst and best birthday of her life.

That night, we all gathered around, even Jeanne and Henri

Valat, to hear what had happened to Papa and how he had eluded the Milice.

It was true that there was another informer in the village, besides the town crier. The Resistance suspected someone but could not be sure of how much the informer knew, or how many families had been denounced. The supervisor at the factory had warned all the Jewish men who worked there to cut their shifts short that afternoon and go home. He believed there was to be an inspection.

Papa had hurried out of the place and made his way back to Arthès, following the secret route he always took whenever there was trouble in the village.

The information network between St. Juéry and Arthès was so sophisticated that minutes after the first Resistance member had noticed the police car enter the village of Arthès, a man was sent to warn Papa at the factory. Several other Resistance members posted themselves at each entrance to the village so that they could warn Papa in case he was already on his way home.

Just as Papa entered the village, he caught sight of Madame Federer, another refugee, who was walking straight toward him. They met on the corner of our street, and Madame Federer told Papa to run away.

"What's happened?" Papa asked her.

"The police were just here," Madame Federer replied. "They asked me if I knew about a Monsieur Kapp. I told them there were many new people in the village, and I didn't know who they were talking about."

"Where did they go?" Papa asked.

"I told them to go to the townhouse. Don't go home, Monsieur. You don't have time. Hide!"

"So," Papa told us, "what could I do?" Madame Federer had seen the police on the street; there was no possibility of going home, or even of hiding out at the Fedous. No doubt their apartment would also be searched and they would be questioned.

"Where did you go, Papa?" I finally asked.

"I hid in the latrines!"

"You mean you were right there, right across from our apartment?"

Papa laughed. "Lucky for me, the police did not have the urge to come in while I was there hiding!"

Madame Valat and I started giggling. "You've been hiding there all this time?" Maman wanted to know.

"No, no. I climbed up to the attic above the latrines and watched at the little window until I saw them leave. Then I waited another quarter of an hour or so before I ran into the fields. I hid there until it was past dark. I'm afraid the four of us all fell asleep. It's quite peaceful there, under the stars."

"The four of you?" Monsieur Valat asked.

"Yes. They were looking for Oscar Nussbaum, Joseph Kahn, and the new one, Monsieur Dimmardman, along with me. Dimmardman told the police he had to go get something and never returned. We met him later in the field!"

"Fortunately," Madame Valat said, "the wheat is high!" and we all laughed again.

Maman wanted to know whether the Milice had come directly to Uncle Oscar's and Monsieur Kahn's houses in St. Juéry. If so, then they, too, would no longer be safe there.

"I don't know about Oscar," said Papa. "He had been gone all morning, and Michel had been out looking for him. He finally found Oscar just getting off the bus! He had made a very dangerous trip to Albi to buy a present for Lissy's birthday!"

"*Really?* He's a fool," cried Maman.

"But wait 'til you hear about Monsieur Kahn," Papa continued. "They came to his house while he was still there!"

"What happened to him?" we all asked at once.

"He was escaping out the bedroom window at the same moment that the police were breaking down the front door. Madame Kahn pretended to be irate, as though she and Joseph had just been having an argument. 'What do you want?' she asked the police. They told her they were looking for her husband.

"'Give me your gun!' she demanded. 'If anyone's going to shoot my husband, it's going to be me!'

"Then, she turned and yelled in the Alsatian dialect for Joseph to get out of there fast. The police did not understand her. She was stalling for time until he could jump from the roof to the street and hide."

"And they never saw him?"

"No. He was already long gone by the time they searched the bedroom."

"Madame Kahn—she's incredible!" Maman exclaimed. "It's a wonder they didn't turn the gun on her!"

I asked Papa how he could possibly have known that we were at the Valats' house.

"I came up the street the back way," he said, "through the gardens. Andrée Fedou was out there, waiting for me. Somehow, she guessed I'd come back that way. She brought me here."

Maman shook her head. "That girl is going to get herself caught if she is not careful."

It was true that the Fedous had taken great risks for us ever since we had moved to Arthès. Monsieur Fedou kept zealous watch over us. At that moment, he was probably searching the village for a place to hide Uncle Oscar and Joseph Kahn.

"We are very fortunate," Maman said, as she always did whenever we had narrowly escaped disaster.

"No," Papa contradicted her with a sober look in his eyes. "It is more than just good fortune."

Monsieur Valat looked across the dim room at Papa. "Yes," he said, "here you have a man who seems to possess an uncanny sixth sense. He has always been able to stay one step ahead of disaster."

Papa suddenly put his arm around me and held me close. "But it was Renée who helped save me today," he said. "She stalled the police and gave me time enough to hide."

Was that what I had done? All afternoon, I had convinced myself that, in some small way, I was responsible for attracting the attention of the French police. How else had they known who and where I was? Why had they first come to me to ask about Papa?

But now, here was Papa telling me he was proud of me; and Maman, for the first time during the period that we had been in hiding, told me that I was a brave girl.

Madame Valat brought down quilts for us to sleep on, and then she and her husband said good night to us. In spite of the fact that they were putting themselves in danger by hiding us, the Valats were gracious, cheerful, and perhaps rather glad to have company in the house. When Madame Valat turned out the light above our heads and then closed the door at the top of the stairs, I buried my face in the quilt. It was too dark even to look for the face of the man with the chipped tooth. Yet I knew he was there. I felt him watching us, waiting for another time, perhaps when I was left alone in the dark, to capture me.

It was all so contradictory: the police could have taken me when they did not find Papa or Maman. That would have been a way to draw my parents to the police station. Yet they had left me alone.

Maman and Papa talked for a long time that night. Maman was frightened to go back to our own apartment room. She was now convinced that we had to move away from Arthès altogether.

"But where will we go?" Papa asked simply.

Except for Aunt Sophie and Jeannette in Toulouse, we had no family in any other part of France, and there was no possibility of our returning to Toulouse.

"At least here the people care about us," Papa mumbled. "Could we find a community like this somewhere else?"

By morning, my parents had decided on a plan. Papa was soon to go away, alone, perhaps for several months. Neither he nor Maman would tell me where he was going. I knew that it must be a place that the Resistance had found for him. All my parents would say was that it was a safe place, a place where the Milice would never know to look for him.

A Drive in the Country

We stayed at the Valats' house for a week or two more. Now that we were hiding in earnest, Maman kept me home from school, despite the fact that Madame Sachs could no longer come out to tutor me. She, too, was now terrified of being discovered and taken away.

When the Protestant minister came to see Papa at the Valats', I realized that he was most certainly one of the ones involved in arranging for Papa to go away. They talked for an hour down in the cellar. Maman and I went up to the kitchen with Madame Valat, and I was allowed to help her bake bread. Maman said the minister was helping Papa make plans, but when the man finally left, I hated him for trying to take Papa away from us, and I began to cry.

Papa came up to the kitchen and sat next to me at the table. He explained that the longer he stayed with us, the more trouble we would have from the authorities who were looking for Jewish men. The minister had told Papa that Maman and I would be safer in the village if he were gone.

"Where will you go, Papa?" I asked, wiping my eyes.

"To a farm. I am going to live with a farmer in the mountains."

"Benno!" Maman cried. "You shouldn't tell her anything! If anyone ever asks her where her father is—"

"They already did once, and she handled them very well, didn't she?" Papa smiled. "I would rather she have some idea where I am than spend every day that I'm gone wondering about me. She knows enough not to say anything," he reassured her.

"Why can't Maman and I go to the mountains with you, Papa?" I asked. I had never lived in the mountains, and I was tired of living in the Valats' cellar. Perhaps in the mountains, we could live in a house of our own.

"It would be too difficult for us all to travel together," Papa explained. "Besides, this farmer, he will not have room for an entire family. You and Maman will be safe here, and the Valats and the Fedous will look after you. Once the war is over, I will come back for Maman and you, and we can live anywhere we want."

"What if it's never over?"

Madame Valat laughed. "It will be over soon, Renée," she said. "I can tell from the radio reports. Don't worry, your father will be safe."

But Madame Valat's prediction was small comfort to me. That night, after we ate, I watched Maman pack Papa's clothes in a bag. I sat in the corner on a sack of potatoes and cried, having no idea when I would see Papa again, if ever. He might never come back. How did he know that he could trust the minister?

Madame Valat brought down some cheese, bread, and nuts for Papa's journey. Even Monsieur Valat came down and offered Papa a bottle of good wine and some books from his collection for Papa to read once he got to the farm. Papa said he was still not very good at reading in French, but he would gladly accept the wine.

Before he went to sleep, Papa told me a long story. It was a new story I had never heard before about someone who had the same name as me—Ruth. Papa told me that the story took place many years ago. I wondered how the woman in the story could have my name; we had not met anyone else in France who was called Ruth. In the story, this woman, Ruth, was married to a Hebrew man who was from Bethlehem, in Judah. Along with his brother and their mother, this man had been living in a country called Moab, because a famine had come to their own land, and it was not possible for them to live there anymore.

When Ruth's husband died, she chose to follow her mother-in-law, who was called Naomi, back to the land of Judah. She left her own father and mother, and her native land, and went to live among people she had never known before—her husband's people. In the new land, Ruth was respected and honored by all who came to know her, and especially by one of her relatives, who was called Boaz. When Ruth married Boaz and bore him a son, Naomi was overjoyed to have a family once more, and gave thanks to God. Ruth's child was named Obed, and he was to be the grandfather of the great King David.

When Papa finished, he kissed me and said that the story would one day make sense to me. He said that I would remember the story, and would understand why he had told me the story on that day. Although I knew about King David, I had not heard of the other characters before. I was too tired to ask Papa more and soon fell asleep.

In the morning, when I woke up, Papa was gone.

Several days after Papa's departure, when Madame Valat had heard that it would be safe for us to return to our own apartment, Maman and I thanked the Valats once more, packed our clothes, and walked back to our street at dusk. Our apartment was just as we had left it, since the Fedous had kept it clean during our absence. In that room above the *tabac*, Maman and I lived alone, without Papa, as we had done in Alençon three years before. It was there, sometime after we had returned to the apartment, that I began to have nightmares. I would wake with a start to find myself lying in the pitch-black room, listening to silence.

One night, I lay awake, but with my eyes shut tight against the black void of the room. We kept the dark green shutters fastened at the windows from dusk until dawn, so that at night, without the comforting shadows of the street, the room was transformed into a stifling, empty space, much like the Valats' cellar. I remember opening my eyes and staring into the dark until the shapes of the room gradually became clear to me, and then I saw Maman sitting at the kitchen table, her hands folded, thinking. She hardly moved and did not know that I was awake. I could tell she must be worrying about Papa.

We had never felt so exposed to danger, and with Papa gone, Maman must have felt overwhelmed with the responsibility of caring for me and keeping me safe. Those days, Monsieur Fedou came and went; we were never sure when we could count on his presence for protection. Sometimes he had to go into hiding himself. Madame Fedou had told Maman that the Milice were beginning to arrest women and children all around us. My uncle lived a village away, and there was no one we could count on to look after us. Still, in the daylight, whenever I asked Maman about the police, her answers convinced me that nothing would ever happen to us, that we were safe. "As long as I am here, Renée, no one will hurt you or take you away from me," she promised.

One afternoon, Madame Kahn and Aunt Hanna came to visit Maman. They had brought Emmy and Evelyne with them, and the three of us played games on the apartment floor while Maman talked with her friends. I did not listen closely to what they were saying, but I heard Maman tell Madame Kahn about Papa's departure to the farm. I heard her say, "Espéreusse, *dans la Montagne Noire* [in the Black Mountain]" and realized that must be the place where Papa was hiding.

Madame Kahn began to tell Maman about another place she had heard of, but I did not pay attention. I remember bits of their conversation, words that were foreign and indistinguishable, and other words—*le couvent* (the convent) and *les religieuses* (the nuns)—that I could not place in the context of their talk.

As Maman listened, she was watching me intently; at first, she shook her head, as though refusing to consider something that Aunt Hanna and Madame Kahn had proposed. I heard her say, "I will think about it, I will. But I can't bear the thought!"

When it grew dark, Madame Kahn and Aunt Hanna walked back to St. Juéry with their children. As soon as they had left, Maman made dinner for me and then told me I must go to bed early. This seemed strange, since I had lately been allowed to stay up much later, especially during the time we stayed with the Valats. Sometime during the night, I heard footsteps crossing the wooden floor, and then I felt Maman's presence near my bed. I knew that she was looking down at me, but she did not know that I was awake, and I did not open my eyes. I felt her draw the sheet up around my shoulders to cover me, and then she lay down next to me. I could not even hear her breathing; it was as if she held her breath so as not to wake me. A little while passed, and when I turned, Maman put her arm around me and held me close. When I reached to touch her face with my hand, it was wet with her tears. "Go to sleep," she murmured.

In the morning, I ran down to the pump for our water. Once Papa's job, this errand had become mine when Papa no longer could go out into the street. Maman told me never to talk to anyone on my way to and from the pump, and never to mention what had happened to Papa. To anyone who asked, I was to say that Papa had been taken away by the Milice in the last roundup.

Maman and I washed at the basin in our apartment as on any other day, and then I helped her sweep the floor. It was then, as we finished tidying the room, that Maman asked me how I would like to spend my day. Before I had time to answer, she told me that the Kahns were going on a vacation and had invited me to go along.

"What about you?" I asked Maman.

"I'll be here when you get back," she told me.

"When will I get back?"

"I'm not sure. That's really up to the Kahns." Maman looked away and began folding some of my clothes. "It's a drive of about 95 miles [150 kilometers]. You'll like the drive, Renée. It's out in the country."

I thought it must be very far from Arthès. "Is it near Papa?" I wanted to know.

Maman laughed. "No, Renée. But wouldn't you like to have some fun on vacation with Emmy? You'll be able to play outdoors again." Maman told me that Emmy was a good friend and that I should accompany her on the trip since she had been kind enough to invite me. I agreed. I told Maman that I would go.

We packed some of my clothes in a bag, and Maman brushed my hair. It did not occur to me, at that point, to ask Maman why she was packing so many of my clothes when I was only going to be gone for a few days.

We left our apartment and walked toward St. Juéry. I felt strange, walking in the open air, without that feeling of having to dart from house to house. Since I had no brothers or sisters, I was excited and looking forward to spending time with Emmy and Jean-Claude. When we got to the Kahns' house, I saw that Aunt Hanna was there, too, but there was no sign of Uncle Oscar, nor of Raymonde and Evelyne. I wondered why they were not going on vacation with us.

A small black car was parked in the street in front of the Kahns' house. I had never seen it before and was afraid at first that it might belong to a German soldier. But Maman did not seem worried, and, as we drew closer, I saw that Emmy and Jean-Claude were already sitting in the backseat; they, too, had brought bags of clothes. Emmy was wearing several layers of clothing, although it was a warm day, and at the last minute, Maman pulled a sweater out of my bag and put it around my shoulders. Then she hugged and kissed me and said, "Be careful and be a good girl, Ruth," as she pushed me into the car. I saw tears in her eyes, and she held her hand to her mouth.

"Maman—" I started to say.

"*Bonnes vacances!*" she cried, and then she waved, trying to smile.

Madame Kahn hurried around to the front of the car, opened the door, and got in. In a moment, the car was running. Maman and Aunt Hanna waved and wished us a good vacation once again, and we all waved back as the car pulled away, headed toward Albi. I thought I would be seeing Maman in a day or two, so I did not turn around to wave goodbye to her one last time.

Madame Kahn was an attractive, talkative woman, but the last few times that I had visited her with Maman she seemed nervous and preoccupied. That morning, as she drove off down the main street, I was aware of how rigidly she sat in the seat and clenched the steering wheel. She looked to her left and right constantly.

"Where did you get this car, Maman?" Jean-Claude asked.

Madame Kahn explained that someone in the Resistance had provided us with the use of the car for only a day.

"Then how will we get home?" I wanted to know.

"Don't worry about that, Renée. People will come to get us."

We followed the main road, in the direction of Albi. I saw signs indicating the number of kilometers left before we reached the town. I remember little else about that excursion through the warm November morning. I talked and laughed with Emmy and Jean-Claude, and we played guessing-games, but Madame Kahn told us to keep our voices down; she had to concentrate on the road. Occasionally, she consulted a piece of paper on which someone had drawn a map for her.

We passed brown fields that suddenly came alive: a sea of yellow butterflies took flight in a strong breeze, huge cows grazed along the sides of the road, and in the distance great patches of weeds and wildflowers shuddered in the wind. Madame Kahn brushed her bright red hair away from her face and squinted at the road. She had worn glasses before the war but had lost them while in hiding, and now she couldn't afford another pair.

She was driving very fast, as though pursued. The man who

had offered her the use of the car worked in the post office in Albi. Unknown to his coworkers, he was also a member of the Resistance network. He had cautioned Madame Kahn about road checks; very few people had the use of a car in those days, and those who did found it nearly impossible to obtain gas rations. For the most part, cars were used by government officials, or by collaborators, who had little trouble acquiring rations from the Germans. Should Madame Kahn be stopped by the police, she was to tell them that her friend at the post office had loaned her the car to visit an ailing relative. The Kahns had false papers, and the man at the post office had supplied Madame Kahn, illegally, with a special pass to drive the car.

I am not sure at what moment it finally dawned on me that I had no idea where we were going. I had never been on a vacation before, but there was such a sense of urgency that morning that we reach our destination. I felt a sickening sensation deep in my stomach. Why had Maman not told me how long I would be away?

As we drove through Albi, we stared out of the windows at the red-tiled roofs of the houses, and at the enormous Cathedral of Sainte-Cécile. This was the cathedral we had passed on our way through Albi, in the darkness, that first night of our arrival. The cathedral was unlike any building I had ever seen; it was constructed entirely of brick, and there appeared to be a fortress surrounding the cathedral itself. Madame Kahn drove along the cobblestone street and crossed a broad square. She intended to stop at the cathedral, but I did not know why.

As soon as she had parked the car close to the side of the cathedral, Madame Kahn hurried us out and led us up a long flight of wide stone steps to a broad wooden door. Standing there at the top of the steps, we had a view of the entire town of Albi and, in the distance, the river Tarn.

"Hurry children, hurry. We don't have much time," Madame Kahn urged.

"What are we doing here?" Jean-Claude demanded.

"There is something I want to show you."

Inside, the cathedral was dark and seemed to go on forever. Our footsteps echoed as we walked through the nave. I felt as if I were back in the dark, cavernous church in Toulouse where Jeannette and I used to hide. Madame Kahn seemed to know exactly what she wanted us to see. We followed her past frescoes and paintings until we came to a statue of a woman wearing a long dress. This statue was not all white, like the one of the woman in the church in Toulouse. This woman was painted in different colors. She had a crown on her head, and she was beautiful.

Madame Kahn murmured, "This is a statue of Queen Esther, children. You know the story of Esther, the one who saved the exiled Jews from the massacre at the hands of the terrible Haman." She was talking primarily to Jean-Claude, who was older and familiar with the story. "Haman tried to destroy the Jews as the Nazis are now trying to do. It is because of Queen Esther that we have our feast called Purim," she went on. "Do you remember Purim?"

We all nodded, although I had no memory of Purim. Madame Kahn was talking in a very soft voice and looking all around us as if someone might be listening. But the cathedral was dark inside, and we were hidden in the shadows.

"Whatever happens," Madame Kahn went on, "remember that you are Jewish. Do not speak of it to anyone, but never forget it. Be proud of it, as Queen Esther was."

Then she hurried us back through the nave and over to the door, where we quickly filed out. We ran down the steps and over to the car. Madame Kahn followed one of the main roads out of town. We crossed the Pont Vieux, the oldest bridge in France. As we drove, I remember wondering why Madame Kahn had made such a point of taking us to the cathedral to show us the statue of Esther. It would be better, it seemed to me, if we could forget altogether about being Jewish. Jewish people got into trouble and were taken away. If Haman had tried to get rid of the Jews, and now the Nazis, under Hitler, had the same intention, there must be something terribly wrong with being Jewish. We had false papers, and by pretending we were not Jewish we'd be able to stay alive. Jeannette had emphasized so many times that I must never, ever admit that I was Jewish. Inwardly, I decided to forget what Madame Kahn had said.

I saw signs for Castres and Carcassone. I leaned forward and stared out the window, trying to remember everything about the trip in case I had to find my way home again. If we didn't have the use of the car to get back, we might have to walk all the way, or find someone who would drive us. I would have to remember as many landmarks as I could.

A shrill burst of laughter erupted from the backseat. Jean-Claude was making gruesome faces while Emmy giggled and turned away. Their laughter annoyed me. I wanted to go home.

Madame Kahn brought the car to a stop along the side of the road at the edge of a wooded area. She told us we had only a few minutes to stop and eat lunch. She looked at her watch over and over. I could tell that she was tired of driving. Her eyes were hurting, she said. There was an old curtain that someone had left in a heap in the back of the car, and we spread this over the grass and sat down to eat the bread and cheese that Madame Kahn had brought for our trip. We were tired and thirsty, but there was very little water left.

"Where are we going?" Emmy asked her mother.

"To a place in the country," Madame Kahn answered, impatient to be back on the road. "You'll like it. It's safe there."

"Why didn't Papa come with us?"

"He had other things to do today."

Jean-Claude had run off into the woods. Madame Kahn stood up and called for him, but he did not return for a while. When he did, he was looking down, a sad expression on his face. I believe Madame Kahn must have told him, in private, where she was taking us, but she had made him promise not to tell us. Emmy and I looked at each other but we didn't talk as we finished our bread. Something was wrong—we could feel it—but we were afraid to ask questions, afraid even to guess what was happening to us. All I knew was that Maman was not there and that I should never have left her. What if she went to find Papa without me? Perhaps they were trying to get rid of me.

We all stood up and shook out the curtain, then climbed back into the old black car. Jean-Claude sat in the front seat with his mother; Emmy and I were in the back. We were on the road, the only car to be seen for several kilometers. Madame Kahn must have thought we were asleep in the back, because I heard her say to Jean-Claude in a low voice, "You are going to have to be very brave now, Jean-Claude, and take care of your sister."

I was afraid and closed my eyes. Who would care for me?

I am leaning against the car window. The window is open slightly, and I feel a cool breeze across my face. I think of sitting up and looking out the window, but I'm too tired. We've been driving for a long time, almost all day, but we cannot stop. Madame Kahn told us we would not stop again until we reached our destination.

I have already missed many landmarks because I fell asleep. Now I will never be able to get home. I will have to ask someone for help; perhaps Jean-Claude will help me, too, when he is taking care of Emmy. He has been watching out the window all along. Whenever I close my eyes, I can see Maman standing on the street outside the Kahns' apartment, waving to me. But I cannot see Papa's face unless I don't think about it. Sometimes, when I'm thinking of something else, his face will come; I will just remember how he looks. But if I try to hold on to the image, it's gone again. I hope it won't be like that with Maman. I can even see the bright print of her dress. Little blue and green flowers. She was going to make a dress for me out of the same material, and she said I needed some new petticoats.

Emmy is awake, too. The car slows down. Emmy leans toward the window. We pass a road sign that says "SORÈZE." We turn down a broad street, and then another corner, and we are on a narrow street. There is a hill in the distance, but the grass is no longer green.

Madame Kahn stops the car. "This is the place," she says. "They told me to stop here. Soon the nuns will come for us."

I do not know what nuns are. Jean-Claude sits up. He is anxious. We are all looking in the same direction, down the street. In the distance, I see a courtyard and a stone wall surrounding the courtyard. It is very high. There is a tall stone building, with long narrow windows. The windows have glass of different colors. Jean-Claude says, "It looks like a castle!" A man on a bicycle passes our car and nods at Madame Kahn. I do not then realize that he is with the Resistance and has been posted on this street in order to signal us when it is safe to get out of the car.

Madame Kahn opens the car door and gets out.

"Come on, Emmy, Renée, it's time to get out," she says firmly. I am afraid to look at her face. I see her taking my bag out of the car. She hands it to me.

"Where are we, Maman?" Emmy asks.

Madame Kahn smoothes her hand over Emmy's hair and bends down to button her sweater. "I have to leave you here for a while, Emmy. You'll be safe here with Jean-Claude. This is a convent, and the nuns here are going to take care of you until I can come back for you."

"But, Maman!" Emmy cries. "Why can't you come, too?"

"I am not allowed to go in today. Don't worry. You won't be alone. I'll come visit you. As soon as it's safe again, you children can come home."

Madame Kahn has been talking all along to Emmy. At first, I think I am not going to be left. I will get to go home to Maman. My legs are trembling. I suddenly feel sick.

Emmy rushes to her mother and clings to her legs. She is crying. I start to cry, too. Jean-Claude stands with his hands in his pockets. He doesn't say anything. He has to be brave.

"I'll be good, Maman," Emmy cries. "Please can't we go home with you?"

But Madame Kahn pries Emmy's hands free, lifts her up into her arms, and says, "Bring your bags and follow me. No one must see us. Hurry!"

I want to ask about Maman. When can I see her? Why didn't she bring me here? But it's too late. Madame Kahn takes my hand, and Jean-Claude is following behind us. We hurry down a sidewalk. Emmy has stopped crying. We've come to a wooden door in the middle of a stone wall. Jean-Claude rings the bell. A man opens the gate and says they are expecting us. "The sisters are just finishing afternoon prayer," he says. He is dressed in old clothes; he looks as if he might be the gardener. Then a lady comes. She is dressed in black—a long black dress of heavy material. There is black material over her head. It looks as if she has no hair. Her sleeves are wide and long. I let go of Madame Kahn's hand and back away. She puts Emmy down, then pushes the three of us forward as she addresses the lady in black. "These are my children," she says, wiping tears away from her face. "Emmy and Jean-Claude."

The lady nods, smiling, and her veil blows in the wind. I've never seen anyone dressed like this. I don't know what to do. I could run into the fields, I think, and I start to turn away, but Madame Kahn says, "Come here." She takes me by the hand. "Here is my other daughter, Renée. She's a bit upset. She doesn't understand."

I look up into Madame Kahn's face. Why has she lied? I am not her daughter. Has she stolen me away from Maman? I cannot move; my legs are weak. I want to run back up the street or into the trees, but I feel I am going to sink into the dirt. The lady takes my hand. Madame Kahn kisses Emmy and Jean-Claude one last time, and she says she will see them on Sunday. She doesn't kiss me. Does the lady think it's strange?

"Come with us!" Emmy screams, but her mother turns away and hurries back up the street. She has not even told me when I can see Maman. She has left us in the street. I can hear the sound of the car starting up and driving away.

The lady nudges us through the door, and we are standing in the middle of a courtyard. She bolts the door behind us.

"Follow me, children," she says. She has a soft voice. No one ever tells us the lady's name.

We walk at a fast pace, following the sidewalk that goes around the courtyard walls. There is gravel in the middle, white stones that make a crunching noise as we walk on them. There is no one else in the courtyard. The lady keeps her head bent. Her arms are folded in her wide black sleeves. "Don't cry, Emmy," she says. "You'll be safe here. You will like it. We are going to take good care of you." Emmy and I do not look at each other. We are holding hands.

We follow the lady across the gravel to a building. It is called the convent. Everything is dim inside; there are candles in little holders and a few lamps on the walls. The lady leads us to a wooden bench in the parlor. "Wait here," she says. We sit down. The floor is newly waxed. The lady goes into a room and we hear voices. She is talking to someone about us. I hear her say our names very slowly and very deliberately. Her voice is soft and light.

When she comes back into the hall, the lady says, "Here is Sister Marie Louise." She turns to another lady who is dressed in the same strange way. "Do what she asks of you, children, and do not be afraid." Then the lady tells us goodbye. She shakes our hands. The black material on her head falls forward over her shoulder like hair. I look up into her blue eyes and they seem to be smiling at me, though her mouth is not smiling. When she walks down the hall, the black veil flows back and forth. She is Mother Superior. We will not speak to her again for weeks.

The other one, Sister Marie Louise, takes our bags. She is very tall, with a wide face and severe eyebrows. "Follow me," she says. "There will be no talking in the corridors." She speaks in a strange accent. We discover later that she is from Spain.

She leads us to the other end of the corridor and then up a

flight of stone steps. She tells us that we have missed the afternoon lessons for the day. "You will be in my class," she tells Emmy and me as we turn into a narrow passage. "Now stop crying, Emmy. You don't want everyone to think you're a cry-baby, do you?"

"I want to go home! I want Maman!" Emmy tells her.

The woman shakes her head. "You have no parents," she says.

"Yes, we do!" Jean-Claude insists. "We just left Maman in the street. She drove away in the black car! Didn't you see her?"

The woman stops walking and glares at Jean-Claude, an angry expression on her face. "Here, we do not tell stories, young man."

Jean-Claude is silent, but I can tell he already hates Sister Marie Louise. She thinks Jean-Claude is a liar. I break away from Emmy and run back down the stairs, but there is another lady coming up. She stops me, her hands on my shoulders. "No running in the corridors, Mademoiselle!" She is also dressed in black, and she leads me back up the passage.

"Some of our new students?" she asks Sister Marie Louise.

"Yes. And not very pleased to be here."

The lady nods.

"You take the boy to his dormitory," Sister Marie Louise orders. "I will take care of the girls."

We do not know what the word "dormitory" means, and we are terrified for Jean-Claude. In a moment, he is gone. We are afraid we will never see him again. We do not ask about him, for the lady might tell us, "You have no brother." Sister Marie Louise takes Emmy and me by our hands. We carry our bags. She is leading us down another dark corridor. We've entered a new building. You can get from the convent into this building on the inside. The windows in the walls are narrow and too high up for me to see outside. I know we will never be able to find our way back into the street. We stop before a wooden door. "This is where you will sleep," Sister Marie Louise tells us.

She opens the door with a key that is tied to her belt, then takes our bags and leads us into a long, dark room. There are rows of white cots on either side. We walk to one end of the room, and Sister Marie Louise points to one of the cots. "That's yours," she says to me. Beside the cot, there is a little table. There is a locker against the wall, dividing my bed from the next one. I'm supposed to share the locker with someone else. Emmy's cot is on the other side of the room, under a window. We are not allowed to talk to each other unless it is absolutely necessary. They are going to separate us. It leaves an empty feeling in my stomach. The lady unpacks our clothes and hangs them up in our lockers.

"What? Haven't you a coat?" she asks. "Only this sweater?"

I nod.

"That is not how you are to answer," she tells me. Her face is stern. "You must say, 'Yes, Sister, this is all I have.'"

"Yes, Sister," I repeat. "Maman forgot to give me my coat."

"My dear child, you must not talk about your mother. She is no longer here. You are an orphan; that is why you have come to us. This is an orphanage."

I do not say anything. I do not know what an orphan is. Tears are starting in my eyes.

"Well," Sister Marie Louise continues, "I don't know what you'll do when winter comes. We'll have to find you a coat soon. Here in the mountains, the winters are fierce."

The words almost cause me to faint: "when winter comes." Does she think I will be here that long? Doesn't she realize this is all a mistake, that I do not belong in this place? What would Maman say? What would Maman tell me to do?

"Now, get undressed. Both of you will have to bathe before dinner. You first," she tells me.

At the end of the room, there is a white door leading into another room. Sister Marie Louise goes into it, and we hear water pouring as we undress. I stand in my slip and underwear. The room is so cold, I wrap my arms around myself. Sister Marie Louise comes out and hands me a towel and a washcloth. She opens the white door and pushes me inside, leaving the door slightly open. Inside, there are two parts to the bathroom. On one side, there is a row of showers with curtains in the front. On my side, there is a tub filled with warm water.

"Be quick!" the lady calls. She can hear me inside.

I climb into the tub and splash water over myself. It is so cold in the bathroom that steam rises from the warm water. There is a cube of soap on the ledge. I rub it over my knees, my arms, my chest. I start to cry, but I cover my face with the washcloth so the lady can't hear me. Maman used to bathe me at home. Now, I am alone. Who will look after me?

"Finished?" asks Sister Marie Louise in her strange accent. I go out, wrapped in the towel. "You next," she tells Emmy. The nun goes into the room, and we hear the water pouring again while Emmy is undressing. When she comes out, she pushes Emmy through the door. Then she notices my clothes.

"No! No! No!" she cries. "You do not put on your soiled clothes that you have been traveling in. You have just bathed! You must put on a clean dress for dinner!" She looks in my locker at the clothes. "Here. Put this on," she commands. It's a plaid dress. It used to belong to Jeannette when she was a little girl. Aunt Sophie gave it to me when we still lived in Toulouse. It is my favorite dress. I think of Jeannette and almost feel her presence with me when I put it on. Sister Marie Louise combs my hair. She throws my dirty clothes into a basket on the floor. I wonder what will happen to them.

When Emmy comes out, Sister Marie Louise helps to dress her and combs her hair. "Are you girls hungry?" she asks us.

We shake our heads.

"No, Sister," she instructs.

"No, Sister," we repeat.

"Well nevertheless, it is almost time for prayers and supper. You may lie down on your cots for a few minutes, and I will come back for you shortly." Then she is gone. I hear her turn the key in the latch. We are locked in.

I bury my face in my pillow. I cannot swallow. When Sunday comes, will Maman come with Madame Kahn? How will I find my way through the corridors out into the courtyard before Sunday? I will have to wait until no one is around. I promise myself I will not talk to anyone because they will tell me I have no parents, that my parents are dead.

Emmy comes over to my bed. We have both been crying.

"Who is going to take care of us?" she asks me.

"I don't know."

We sit on the edge of the bed together, waiting for Sister Marie Louise to come back for us. We are holding hands, talking as quietly as we can.

"I wonder what will happen to Jean-Claude," I whisper.

"I don't know. Maybe he will be allowed to eat with us."

"Do you think your mother will come back to get us on Sunday?"

"Yes, I think so. Maybe this is our vacation and it will only last a week. I think Sunday is visiting day. Then we will go home."

"I hope so. I don't like it here."

"No."

Other children are filing into the dormitory. Sister Marie Louise is at the door, hurrying them inside. We do not say a word. We stand by my cot and cling to its metal frame. Some of the girls wash their hands at the sinks in the far corner of the room. They are giggling. Sister Marie Louise insists that all those who have not washed their hands must do so. She is our "dormitory mother." She checks Emmy's hands, then mine, and tells us to get in line with the others.

"Silence!" she calls. "Everyone in line! Next to her partner!"

She tells us to get our prayer books out of the drawers by our beds. I don't know what she means. I follow everyone else. There's a black book in the drawer for me. We are told to hold the books in our right hands, pressed against our chests. Everyone puts a blue béret on her head, but Emmy and I don't have one.

Sister Marie Louise leads us out the door, down the steps, and through the dark corridor. It is a long walk. I can tell we're back in the convent building. The windows are different. We follow the dark corridor to a wooden door. "Shhh!" the nun says. "May I remind you, Mesdemoiselles, that we are about to enter the House of the Lord!"

Everyone's face changes. We all look solemn. Sister Marie Louise opens the door, and I can tell we are inside a church. Jeannette used to tell me that the church was the safest place in Toulouse to hide. There are candles flickering at the front of the church, and statues, standing in the corners of the room, like the one of Queen Esther in the cathedral. All the windows are dark; it is already night. Sister Marie Louise leads us halfway up the aisle. There are wooden benches on either side. Sister Marie Louise points to them and directs us to "our pew." Before we can sit down, we must bend down on one knee and look at the floor. Everyone makes a strange sign with her hand. I don't know what it means, but I remember how the people in the church in Toulouse used to do the same thing when they entered the church and walked up toward the front.

Wordlessly, Sister Marie Louise stops Emmy and me. She bends down with us and shows us how to make the strange sign, which she calls "the sign of the cross." First we touch our foreheads, then our chests, and then our left and right shoulders. She whispers, "In the name of the Father, and of the Son, and of the Holy Ghost, Amen." Afterward, we are not allowed to sit together. Emmy sits on the left side, and I on the right.

As soon as everyone is sitting down, a lady in the front of the church walks into the center and kneels down. It is the lady from this afternoon, Mother Superior. Everyone imitates her and kneels down. We fold our hands, and the lady begins to sing in another language. We are to sing after her, but I cannot find the place in the book. The girl next to me points to the line, but I don't know how to read the language. "It's Latin," the girl says. I pretend I know the right words to sing. This mournful singing lasts a long time. First one side sings, then the other side. Everyone turns the page in the hymnal at the same moment. The song is sad, and I wonder why. Now I know how Maman must have felt going to church with Madame Fedou and Madame Valat.

After the prayers are finished, we follow the corridor to the dining hall, where all our meals will be served.

The dining hall is very big; the ceiling is higher than that of the dormitory. The room echoes with voices. Sister Marie Louise silences us with a clap of her hands. There are long tables, aligned in rows. The boys' tables are at the far end of the hall. We cannot see Jean-Claude anywhere. When the bell rings, there is no sound from the children. We must find a place at a table, but Emmy and I don't know where to go. We hold everyone up by trying to find a place at the benches. When everyone is standing behind her place, another bell rings and another nun starts to talk in a soft voice. We make the sign of the cross again. We press the palms of our hands together and look down at the floor. Emmy and I do it so we won't look different, but we don't know what it means. Everyone says, "Amen."

When we are allowed to sit down, they serve us plates full of food. No one is talking. It is more food than I have ever had at one meal. This can't be for us. I try to eat, but I can't swallow everything as fast as I'm putting it into my mouth. There are mashed potatoes and beans. Sister Marie Louise comes over to me and whispers over my shoulder, "It is a sin to waste food. You must clean your plate and drink your milk." We have to keep eating. Even when all the other girls at the table have stopped eating, I must eat until I have finished everything. Some of the food I have never tasted before. It grows cold on my plate.

At last, the bell rings. We stand up, push in the bench, and say another prayer together. We are conducted out of the hall, back along the cold corridors to our dormitory. Each girl goes to the table beside her bed and puts her prayer book back in the drawer. We begin to undress and wash. I do everything that the other girls do, so I won't stand out. There is a line at each faucet, and I am one of the last to be able to wash. When Sister Marie Louise has inspected our hands, ears, and faces, we go to our beds. Everyone immediately falls to her knees beside her bed. At the sound of another bell, we open the drawers again, each girl taking out a long chain of white beads, but I don't find one of these in my drawer.

I don't know what is happening. Every girl turns to face a wooden cross that hangs on the wall above her bed. There is one above my bed, too. I turn to face the cross, but I don't have the beads, so I just hold my hands together. I look up at the cross. There is the figure of a man hanging on it. It is the same with every cross in the room. There is a long silence, and then Sister Marie Louise and the rest of the girls recite something in unison. I can tell the nun is watching me. My face grows hot. I cannot help it; I do not know the prayers.

Finally, the prayers are over. We touch our foreheads and chests and shoulders, making the sign of the cross once more. Then, each girl slips her chain of beads back in the drawer. Sister says something to us, and then we are allowed to fold back the bedspread and get into bed. The girl next to me says, "You'll have to ask her for a rosary in the morning." I nod, pretending I understand what she means.

The lights go off, and Sister Marie Louise leaves the room. I turn over and hide my face in my pillow. I am afraid everyone can hear my crying. They will laugh and think I am a cry-baby. I wait a long time, until I don't hear a sound. Then I walk to the end of the room and open the white door to the place where we took our baths. I close the door and walk to the window. Here, the windows are low, and I can look out. I can see trees below and part of the stone wall. There are no leaves left on the trees. I think about Maman. How could she have done this to me? Why did she send me to this frightening place? I must be an orphan if it means being all alone, or else she would have come to get me by now. I will never see her again.

The window is so cold that I feel a chill against my face without touching the glass. I go back into the main room, shivering, and climb into the hard bed. But I cannot sleep. I cannot sleep. I cannot fall asleep.

The Convent of Sorèze

It was always cold at the convent in Sorèze. The dormitory walls were stone, as was the floor, and on windy nights the cold air howled through the window frames and the rafters. There was one wool blanket to a bed. After several days, Emmy caught a cold and was taken to the infirmary. One of the nuns brought me a bulky winter coat that had belonged to one of the intermediate students. I was to wear it during recreation in the enclosed courtyard.

We followed a rigid schedule every day. Sister Marie Louise woke us at six-thirty each morning, and as soon as we had washed and dressed, we were taken to the first floor to put on our smocks. Each morning, we went to chapel and were present as the nuns prayed special prayers together. We then had our breakfast in the dining hall. The nuns had already eaten long before. I never knew how to follow the prayers in the black book and was always aware of the other girls watching me.

Every child in the convent was an orphan, or so we

thought. Each time I would ask one of the nuns when I could see my mother, she would tell me, "You have no mother, Mademoiselle. Your mother is in heaven with God. The other children are orphans here, just as you are. You must not be ashamed. You will be taken care of here." I came to believe the nuns. Why would they lie? They kept telling me I had no parents, and after a while I started to give up and wonder if it was true.

I could not eat or sleep during the first week. During classes, I had difficulty concentrating. At first, the nuns who taught me were lenient, but after a while, they would single me out and scold me. "Pay attention, Mademoiselle! Follow the example of your classmates!" When I began to fall behind, I was reprimanded by Sister Marie Louise. She would come over to my desk and ask to see my copy book. Then she would tell me to hold out my hand. I'd hold out my right hand and turn my palm upward, fingers together, as I had seen the other girls do. Then Sister Marie Louise would rap my fingers with her ruler several times. I would feel my face flush with shame, my fingers stinging, but I'd force myself not to cry.

There was something called Holy Mass each morning in the main church. The Mother Superior had explained to Sister Marie Louise that Emmy and I were not Catholics, so she spent several sessions with us explaining what the mass was about.

While we were not to become Catholics ourselves, we were to be instructed in their faith. We learned Catholics believe that Jesus Christ is the Son of God and that He is the Messiah who came into the world to reconcile the world to His Father. It was Jesus Christ who had suffered and died on the cross, and it was through His sacrifice that all sinners are redeemed. The nuns said that the sins of every person are forgiven, and one's relationship with God the Father is restored, through Jesus Christ. We were told that during the mass, Catholics believe this sacrifice of Christ is renewed; the bread and wine the priest has prepared at the altar become the Body and Blood of Jesus Christ. At mass, the other children would go up to the altar rail in a procession, and then would kneel along the rail. The priest would come to each one of them and place a white wafer on her tongue, saying, "Corpus Christi [The Body of Christ]," to which each would respond, "Amen." To the children and the nuns, this was actually the Body and Blood of Jesus Christ they were receiving in the sacrament of Holy Communion.

When Emmy was in the infirmary I would sit in the pew, alone, watching the other girls at the altar rail. Then they would return to their pews, looking down as they walked, their hands pressed together. Each of them wore a white lace veil over her head, but you could see their faces through the veils. It was a solemn moment; they had received the Body of Christ. In the pews, they would bless themselves and cover their faces with their hands.

After dinner we would have evening prayers, called vespers, in the chapel, and then the recitation of the rosary before bedtime. I had been given a string of beads—a rosary— by Sister Marie Louise, who told me to treasure it. She said the rosary was a prayer to Jesus, through Mary, His Blessed Mother. There was a crucifix at the end with which you blessed yourself. I learned to say the Hail Mary prayer, the Our Father prayer, and the Glory Be prayer. I followed all the prayers mechanically; I did it to be accepted and to not stand out. Sometimes, Sister Marie Louise smiled at me. I was called a devout Catholic, but I was only pretending, as Jeannette and I had pretended so many times at the church in Toulouse.

I missed Emmy, particularly during recreation. We were taken out into the courtyard on fair days, and one of the nuns, either Sister Victoire or Sister Présentation, would supervise the games: hide-and-seek, tag, or a Spanish game the nuns called something that sounded like "commados." I was not chosen to be on one of the teams, and, since Emmy was sick, I could not play in the games for which a partner was required. I would sit by the chestnut tree, on one of the stone benches, and watch the others play their games. The boys had their playtime just after ours, and I sometimes caught sight of Jean-Claude coming out the main door, but I could never talk to him.

One afternoon, I saw one of the girls slip and fall on the gravel. She stood up, crying, her knees bruised and bleeding. She was taken immediately to the convent building, which was in the center of the courtyard. I guessed that the infirmary was somewhere inside. That was where they had taken Emmy. I tried to think of ways that I could be sent to the infirmary.

One afternoon during the second week, toward the end of a recreation period, I saw Jean-Claude coming out of the main building with several other boys and the gardener. He had been selected to rake leaves and assist the gardener in trimming the hedges and shrubs. When he saw me sitting on one of the stone benches, he came over to me and whispered, "My mother is coming tomorrow, I think. I'll tell you whatever she says about your parents."

"I think my parents are dead," I told him.

"Why?"

"Because the nuns told me I'm an orphan."

"That's because this is an orphanage, silly. They don't know about us. They think we're like all the other students. Just pretend, and do whatever they say."

"Are you sure, Jean-Claude?"

"Yes! Don't you remember, the Mother Superior talked to Maman in the street? She must have forgotten to tell the other sisters about us."

"Will Emmy get to see your mother?"

"I think so. Maman will have to come to the main building, and that's where Emmy is."

"Young man!" Sister Marie Louise called from the other end of the courtyard. "Get to work!" She clapped her hands together, and Jean-Claude ran back to the gardener.

The next day was Sunday. If I could just get to the infirmary, I would be able to see Madame Kahn when she arrived. She would go up to the infirmary to see Emmy and perhaps Maman would be with her! When Sister Marie Louise called my name, I stood up and started to run toward her. As soon as I reached the gravel, I pretended to slip and actually fell as far as I could across the stones. Sister Marie Louise came over to me and helped me up.

"Are you all right, Mademoiselle? That was the most graceful fall I ever saw!"

I stood up and looked down at my knee. My stocking was torn, but there was no blood, not even a bruise.

"I think you will live, Mademoiselle," the nun said. "Next time, you will remember not to run. Now get in line."

I looked at my knee again and saw that it was red; perhaps a bruise would soon form. I limped toward the line. Sister Marie Louise looked over at me and frowned.

"It hurts when you walk on it?" she asked me.

"Yes, Sister."

She turned to one of the older students, who was called Véronique. "Mademoiselle," she instructed, "take her to the infirmary and wait with her until her knee has been examined by Sister Victoire."

Véronique came out of the line and led me into the main building. Out of the corner of my eye, I saw Jean-Claude watching me. I wanted to let him know that I had faked the whole thing so that I would be able to see Madame Kahn the next day, but I kept limping nonetheless.

Once inside the convent, I remembered the foyer where we had been taken the first day, and the parlor, with its Oriental rugs, where we had waited for Sister Marie Louise. There were no candles flickering that afternoon, and the door to the room where Mother Superior had talked with Sister Marie Louise was closed. Perhaps she was inside. It must be her office.

Véronique took my hand and led me up a flight of wide

wooden steps. It was difficult to pretend to limp on the stairs. As our shoes touched each step, the wood creaked and groaned. At the top of the stairs, on the landing, Véronique turned right and I was taken to a narrow door. She knocked and the nurse, Sister Victoire, opened the door.

The moment I stepped inside, I realized that I was not going to see Emmy. I had been taken to a small office, no bigger than a closet. There were jars on the shelves and boxes of cotton swabs. To the left of the desk, there was a glass cabinet filled with bottles of medicines. The nurse wore glasses and was stooped with age.

Sister Victoire told me to take down my stockings, and then she looked at my knee. She held my calf up and bent the leg, then straightened it. "Does this hurt?" she asked.

I shook my head.

"This?"

"No, Sister."

"It is not broken," she told me. When she saw my face, she laughed and went over to her medicine cabinet. "Very well, I will put a bandage on for you," she said. "That will be more dramatic."

"Thank you, Sister," I said.

As she dabbed the medicine on the bruise and bandaged my knee, I saw that Véronique was leaning forward, staring out the window. The window overlooked the courtyard; we faced the front of the building. Véronique waited until Sister Victoire was finished with my leg, and then she murmured, "Look, Sister. It is the Germans!"

Sister Victoire went to the window. "*Oh, mon Dieu!*" she said, blessing herself. "Nazis!"

Nazi soldiers must have entered the building. I could not see out into the courtyard and had no idea how many there were. Oddly, I didn't feel frightened. Sister Victoire told me to pull up my stockings. "Now, Mesdemoiselles," she said, "hurry back to your classrooms."

We were ushered out of the office and into the hallway. I did not even look for a door marked *l'infirmerie*. I could not guess where Emmy was, but she had to be on the same floor, close to the nurse's office. The moment she left us, Sister Victoire turned down the corridor and went into a room on her left.

Véronique and I hurried down the stairs. As we reached the last steps, we heard male voices—German—issuing from the room on the right, which I was now certain was the Mother Superior's office. Perhaps the Nazis have come for Emmy, Jean-Claude, and me, I thought. Now everyone will know that I am Jewish. Should I try to run away?

"Several convents have already been bombed," one of the officers was saying in French. "Of course, you realize the same fate could be yours."

I looked up at Véronique's face. She had stopped in the foyer and was listening. She looked down at me and held her finger to her lips.

"I assure you," we heard the Mother Superior say, "we have no Jewish children in this convent. This is an orphanage for French children whose parents have been killed in the war. We are quite out of the way, as you see. I cannot imagine how any Jewish refugees would find us."

"Nevertheless," said the officer, "it is conceivable that you, as a member of a religious order, would have responded to the appeal of Archbishop Saliège, requesting that Catholic families and religious institutions offer asylum to the Jews. You would be negligent, to say the least, if you failed to respond to the Archbishop's orders."

There was a moment of silence, then we heard the Mother Superior respond in her soft voice. "Monsieur," she said, "pardon me if I do not address you properly, as I do not know your rank. We, the other religious and myself, are under the direction of the Dominican Friars here at Sorèze. I am sure that if Père Charlet were hiding Jewish children, he would do so at his own discretion. Can you imagine him being so imprudent as to jeopardize the lives of all the other students here at Sorèze, not to mention the friars and the sisters, by taking in Jewish children, knowing what the penalties are? To tell you the truth, we can hardly manage with the number of children we have, what with the food and clothing shortages."

We did not linger to hear any more. Véronique took my hand and led me out of the building. I no longer limped, but walked as fast as I could. As we reached our classrooms, Véronique did not speak to me. She had been trembling ever since hearing the voices of the Nazi soldiers. Perhaps she, too, was Jewish.

All afternoon, I worried that the Nazis might still be on the grounds. Perhaps they would inspect our dormitory, searching for Emmy and me. Worse still, they might return in the morning when Madame Kahn came. Then, I knew, we would all be deported.

In chapel that night, I watched the Mother Superior in the front pew, her head bent, her black veil perfectly even across her back, her big wooden rosary beads at her hip. Surely she knew that Emmy, Jean-Claude, and I were Jewish. Yet the Mother Superior had lied to the German officer.

When the morning came, Emmy was brought back to the dormitory just before high mass. As we were changing into our smocks, I asked her whether her mother had come.

"She cannot come today," Emmy told me.

My heart sank. "Why not?"

"Something has happened. Sister Victoire told me that I would have to go back to the dormitory and couldn't stay in the infirmary anymore. Then the Mother Superior came in to talk to me privately. She told me that I could not see Maman today." Emmy had tears in her eyes.

"When can you see her?"

"I don't know."

"Did she say anything about my mother?"

"No. She thinks we are sisters. She said for me to tell you that we would have to wait longer to see Maman."

I hugged Emmy and almost squealed with happiness. If Emmy's mother was alive, and the Mother Superior had admitted that she had been in contact with Madame Kahn, then my mother could also be alive. Then a thought came to me. "It's because of the soldiers!" I said.

"What soldiers?"

"Germans. They came here yesterday! They talked to Mother Superior and asked her if there were any Jewish children here. She told them there were not. She lied to them."

Emmy didn't say anything. She was looking over my shoulder at one of the girls from my class, who was called Marguerite. She was standing by the washstand. She had heard everything we were saying. Emmy and I fell silent and finished dressing. We got in line with the others and went to Sunday mass. We would have to wait yet another week to see Madame Kahn.

The convent was preparing for Christmas.

It was the beginning of December, and greenery and candles were placed at all the windows. In religion class, I learned about Advent and the birth of Christ. Sister Présentation called on me. "Who were the first visitors to come to the manger in Bethlehem after Jesus was born?" she asked me.

"I don't know, Sister," I murmured.

All the girls in the classroom laughed. This was something everyone else clearly knew, but I was unable to answer. Sister Présentation silenced the class and gave the answer herself: "Of course it was the shepherds, the most humble and lowly people, the least likely to be the first to see the infant King. We know that Jesus chose to be born in such a humble place because He was to be the Good Shepherd of the people, the Savior of the poor, the lowly, the humble of heart."

In the chapel, to the side of the altar, there was a wreath of evergreen branches with red holly berries all around it. Each Sunday, the nuns told us, one of the students would be chosen to light the Advent candle for that week. There were three purple candles and one pink, for the four Sundays of Advent. Each Sunday we were moving closer to the birth of Christ. I was never asked to light one of the candles.

I thought of Hanukkah, the Festival of Lights, when Aunt Sophie had lit candles on the menorah, and Jeannette had explained to me what the Hanukkah lights were. Aunt Sophie had carried the menorah with her, wrapped in linen, all the way from Alsace. She had to keep it hidden all the time. But in the convent, no one mentioned Hanukkah. The Advent candles reminded me of it, however, and I longed to be at home with all my family together. Others talked about the Divine Child who was about to come, but I could not talk about anything.

In religion class one afternoon, each of us was called upon to recite a story from the Bible. The students had studied stories from the Bible all year, but I had never heard of some of the stories before. There was the parable of the mustard seed, and the parable of the sower, the story of the Good Samaritan, the story of the raising of Jairus's daughter, and the story of Jesus walking on water. When my turn came to recite a story, I stood up at my desk. Everyone in the room turned to look at me. For some reason, I began to tell the story Papa had told me before he left for the farm in the mountains, the story from the Book of Ruth. I was able to remember the exact words that Ruth had spoken to her mother-in-law, Naomi, because I had silently said them to Papa and Maman each night since Papa had left:

Wherever you go, I will go,
Wherever you live, I will live.
Your people shall be my people,
and your God, my God.

Wherever you die, I will die
and there I will be buried.
May the Lord do this thing to me
and more also,
if aught but death should come between us.

When I finished, Sister Présentation asked, "Where did you hear this story, Mademoiselle?"

"I do not remember, Sister," I said.

"I see." Sister Présentation turned to the rest of the class. "This story, the story of Ruth, is from the Old Testament, children. It is one we have not discussed before in this class, since we teach the Old Testament later in the year. Most of the stories we have heard today are from the New Testament, from the Gospels. Nevertheless, the story of Ruth is an important one, and you should remember it. Well done, Mademoiselle."

Stunned, I sat down in my chair. I felt my face growing hot. Inwardly, I thanked Papa a thousand times for telling me the story. I wondered, again, whether I had been named for the woman in the Old Testament.

We were all invited to decorate the parlor one afternoon before dinner. A tall cedar tree had been brought in, and there were boxes of ornaments all over the parlor floor. Each student selected two ornaments and placed them on the tree. Mother Superior came in, and we all knelt and watched her place the figurines of Mary and Joseph at the crèche. There was no infant Jesus in the crib yet. He did not get put in the crib until Christmas day.

When the next Sunday came, Emmy and I glanced at each other on and off during Sunday mass. We were both anxiously waiting to see whether Madame Kahn would come, and with her, perhaps, Maman. During our Sunday brunch, I could hardly eat, but my loss of appetite was due to excitement rather than dread.

Younger students at the convent had a nap period every Sunday afternoon. We were expected to sleep or rest quietly on our cots for an hour. I could not sleep. I prayed that Maman would come, and that I would be taken to see her. After our naps, when the other girls were taken to the library for the reading period, the Mother Superior came and took Emmy and me out of line. She told us to follow her down the corridor. In silence, we followed the passage into the convent, our hearts racing. Waiting for us in the foyer were Jean-Claude and two other boys I had never seen before. It was at that moment that I knew I was going to see Maman.

We walked down another long corridor and then up a flight of steps. The stairs were narrow and steep; we must be following the back service stairs, I thought. When we reached the landing, I realized that I was on the same floor as the infirmary. I recognized the narrow door to the nurse's office.

The Mother Superior led us down the corridor in the opposite direction. It was very dark and we could not see anything. We stopped before a wooden door. Mother Superior unlocked the door with a skeleton key.

"You children have forty-five minutes. I will come back for you before dinner." Then she smiled, patted my head, and was gone. The door closed behind us. The first person I saw, seated at a table by the window, was Madame Kahn. She stood up and rushed to Emmy and Jean-Claude, hugging them both. I saw other girls from different classes—there must have been four or five of us—as well as the two boys who had come with Jean-Claude. All of them, I realized, must be Jewish, and all of them were there to see their mothers.

I looked everywhere, but Maman was not there.

Emmy had begun to cry when she saw Madame Kahn, and now she clung to her mother. "Can we go home with you?" she pleaded over and over, but Madame Kahn told us it was still too dangerous in the village.

"Where is my mother?" I asked.

"Poor Renée," Madame Kahn said, pulling me close. She told me Maman could not come that day. "But she is all right, I promise you; she cries for you and thinks of you all the time, Renée. She thinks your father might be able to return to Arthès soon!"

"Why couldn't she come today?" I demanded. "If she is alive, why didn't she come with you?"

"It would have been too dangerous for her. She is not French. You know that. That is why I had to tell the Mother Superior you were my daughter. The orphanage is only for French children. Emmy and Jean-Claude are French, and your mother and I knew you could pass for a French child."

"I want to go back with you today!" I insisted. "I hate it here! If Maman is alive, I have to see her! Why won't you let me?"

Madame Kahn told me not to raise my voice. In a firm tone, she told me I had to be brave. "You children must stay here, where it is safe, until things get better. It is much too dangerous outside. You children have no idea how bad it is. The police are taking people away every week. You must stay here, where you are well fed and can continue with school. Outside, you would not be able to. We are so happy that you are doing so well. Your mother is very proud of you, Renée," Madame Kahn said to me. "She is alive, I promise you. The nuns tell you that you are orphans because all the other children are orphans. Think how much more fortunate you are than they; you will see your Maman again, but those children will never see theirs."

I sat on a chair while Emmy and Jean-Claude talked to their mother, telling her things about the school. I did not say anything. Emmy told Madame Kahn about being in the infirmary, and Jean-Claude asked his mother when she would come again. Madame Kahn could not say. She could come only when she was able to borrow a car. I looked around the stark room at the other children talking to their mothers.

Several of them were in tears. One of them was Marguerite, the girl from our dormitory, who had overheard Emmy and me talking about the German soldiers. She, too, was Jewish.

Madame Kahn had news of Raymonde and Evelyne. She told us that some friends from Alençon had gone into hiding on a farm near Albi. Uncle Oscar and Aunt Hanna had kept in touch with them, and finally had gone to live with them on the farm for a short time. Then, word came that the police were looking for Uncle Oscar. He and Aunt Hanna immediately left the farm and found a one-room apartment in a house that was recessed from the street in Albi. They remained in hiding and were protected by the Resistance. Only Aunt Hanna went out; Uncle Oscar never left the apartment, for fear that he would be picked up by the Milice. Through Uncle Oscar's connections in St. Juéry, Raymonde and Evelyne had been placed in another Catholic convent in Albi.

Madame Kahn gave each of us a candy, and whispered, "Happy Hanukkah, children," as she hugged us goodbye. Then she gave me a little crinkled paper bag. "A present from your mother. She said that you would understand the signal."

I opened the bag and saw that it contained pieces of candy. It was the kind Maman always bought for me! She was alive and had remembered the signal that always let me know that everything was all right. I wondered where she had found them. I would save them for later.

Madame Kahn stood up and went to the door. She had to leave before the forty-five minutes were up, she said, or she would not make it back to St. Juéry before dark. We sat on our wooden chairs, waiting for Mother Superior to return. None of us spoke. We now knew the worst: we had to stay at the convent until the war was over. And no one, not even the Mother Superior, could tell us when that would be.

The Rabbi's Prayer

Each morning, I awoke with an overwhelming feeling of dread, my stomach churning. I felt I could not go through another day without knowing what had happened to my parents. But Maman still did not come to Sorèze. It was too dangerous for her to come.

Although Madame Kahn had assured me that my parents were alive, the nuns were just as certain that they were dead. Several other students also talked about their parents frequently, as though they were still alive, so the nuns finally sat us down one afternoon and told us firmly that we were not to speak of our families anymore. We were all orphans, and there was no point in dwelling on our sadness and our grief, they said. At the convent, we had a new family—our brothers and sisters in Jesus.

Although I now knew who the other Jewish children were at Sorèze, we could never speak to one another about our parents, nor, for that matter, about being Jewish. We had to fit in, and we were afraid we would be reported to Sister Marie

Louise if someone found out that we were Jewish and did not belong. We never spoke the word, unless sure that none of the other children could hear us.

There was an afternoon when Mother Superior came to get us out of class. I met Emmy, Jean-Claude, and several other children out in the corridor. Even Véronique was there. Mother Superior told us to follow her. "Hurry," she said.

We followed her through the corridor and down a flight of steps. We found ourselves outside of the chapel, where there was a narrow wooden door that we had never noticed. Mother Superior unlocked the door and took us down the stairs. Véronique was leading the way. It seemed to me that she had done this before and knew where we were going. We found ourselves in an underground chapel beneath the main chapel. There were several candles in iron stands, a wooden table with a white linen cloth on it, and kneelers on the stone floor. That was all the furniture in the cellar.

Mother Superior told us to sit on the kneelers and to make no noise. "Absolutely no talking, do you hear?" she said.

"Yes, Mother," we responded in unison.

"I'll return for you as soon as it is safe. In the meantime, remember that this is a chapel, and that you must be quiet and respectful," she told us. She left us in the cellar, lighting only one candle on her way out, so that we could see. We heard her returning up the steps, opening the wooden door above, and then shutting and locking it behind her.

"It's the Nazis," Véronique said almost instantly.

"It is?" I asked.

"Yes. This has happened twice before, only you weren't here then. They come and inspect the grounds and all the rooms. This is the only place they don't know about."

Jean-Claude asked, "Have they ever asked to see what is down here?"

"Not yet," Véronique answered.

Some of the other children whispered, but few of us moved

more than a few inches. We listened in the semi-darkness for voices or other sounds that would identify the arrival of Nazi soldiers, but we heard nothing.

Soon, Véronique began to talk again, in a normal voice. "I think it would be easier to give ourselves up," she said. "I'm tired of this hiding. It makes us different. None of the other children have to hide down here."

One of the boys said, "You're stupid. Don't you realize that getting caught means getting killed?"

"Look," Véronique answered belligerently, "I don't care if I get caught. I don't care if I get killed. My parents *are* dead; I know it. I saw them being taken away, in Paris. We lived on a street that had many Catholics. We thought they would not give us away, but I came home from school one afternoon and I saw the Gestapo coming out of the house with Maman and Papa. They couldn't take anything—no clothes, nothing. I ran to the bushes and hid. After they had taken my parents away in the truck, I saw some of our neighbors walking up the steps to our house and opening the door. Nobody had bothered to lock it. I saw the lights go on because it was getting dark out. Then I saw one of the neighborhood ladies coming down the steps wearing my mother's mink coat. And I saw a man riding away, down the pavement on my brother's bicycle. They took everything they wanted. I hate them! They're as bad as the Nazis."

"But nobody's given us away here," I said. "These people are Catholic, and they're hiding us."

"Maybe they are, for now. But somebody will give us away, sooner or later."

We sat in silence, and no one agreed or disagreed with Véronique. She had told her story in anger, yet she was the one who looked the most terrified there in the cellar, as we waited for the Nazis.

After what seemed like several hours, Mother Superior returned to the cellar and told us we could go back to our dormitories. She asked us not to say anything to anyone about where we had been. Véronique turned back, as we were walking up the stairs, and asked Mother Superior if it was the Nazis who had come to the school. "No," the Mother Superior responded. "A false alarm."

There were perhaps one or two other occasions when Mother Superior came into our dormitory, in the middle of the night, and led us back down the service stairs to the cellar-chapel to hide. She waited until all the other children, as well as the nuns, were asleep and then took us down to the underground chapel and left us there for what seemed like hours. On those nights, I realized much later, Mother Superior had undoubtedly been warned to take extra precautions.

One morning, Sister Marie Louise inspected our lockers. When she came to mine, she discovered the little crumpled bag of candies that Madame Kahn had brought for me from Maman.

"Where did you get these?" Sister Marie Louise asked me, holding up the bag of candies for everyone to see.

I shrugged my shoulders. How could I tell her? The Mother Superior had warned us never to mention our visits with Madame Kahn to any of the other nuns or to the other students. "I found them, Sister."

"Mademoiselle," she said, "you know that it is a sin to lie. Did you steal these candies?"

"No, Sister."

"I think you did steal them. I think you took them during the Christmas pageant. There is no other way you could have procured so many! You were told that each child was allowed only one candy, and yet you took an entire handful and hoarded them in your locker."

"No, Sister," I repeated urgently. I was crying. All the girls were listening. Sister Marie Louise was very angry. Her eyebrows were raised, her eyes wide.

"Until you confess what you have done, you will not be permitted to go to dinner."

"I did not take them!" I cried. "They're from my mother! She sent them to me!"

"Mademoiselle," the nun snapped, "you know that you do not have a mother, so she could not possibly have sent them to you. Your mother is in heaven. Now we are all waiting for you to admit what you have done."

I turned and looked at all the faces staring at me. Emmy, too, was crying. I saw Véronique, by the bookcase. She was looking out the window. The sun shone on the gold crown of the statue of the Blessed Virgin that stood in the corner. I knew that it was a sin to lie. If I admitted to having taken the candies, I would be lying. But if I did not admit it, they would never stop staring at me. They would never leave me alone.

"I stole them!" I blurted.

"Yes," said Sister Marie Louise, patting my head, now that I had given in. "And you are sorry for what you have done?"

"Yes."

"Yes, Sister."

"Yes, Sister," I repeated.

"Good. Now wash your face. Let us all get into line for dinner."

I watched Sister Marie Louise tuck the bag of candies away in her deep pocket. I had been saving them, eating one or two when no one could see me. They were the last part of Maman that I had, and now they were gone.

We were led to dinner and I sat at my usual place, not taking my eyes off my plate during the entire meal. I felt the other girls watching me, and I wanted to tell them I had not lied, that the candies were mine, and that my mother was still alive. That night, when I said my prayers, I confessed to God that I had lied, but I did not confess to having stolen. Sister Marie Louise had made me lie.

Madame Kahn came to the convent again after Christmas.

Again, Maman was not with her. This time, there was no candy. There was no sign that Maman was still alive. "The nuns are mean to us," Emmy told her mother. "They say we have no parents."

"Just a little longer, children," was all Madame Kahn could say.

"What about my parents?" I asked. "You tell me they are alive, but I can never see them. The nuns say Maman and Papa are dead—and they are not supposed to lie."

"Renée," Madame Kahn said, "the nuns are speaking out of ignorance. They don't know about us. We have to keep it a secret, for your own protection, so that you will be allowed to stay here. Don't you understand? With you here, your parents are sure that you are safe, and it is easier for them to hide from the police. Sometimes, they have to hide in the fields for days!"

"You mean Papa has come back? He and Maman are together in Arthès?"

"Yes. Doesn't that make you happy?"

"I could hide from the police, too! I know how, I've done it before! I could help them!"

"No, no, no. You do not understand. Your parents cannot even feed you properly. They hardly have enough food for themselves. Here, you have all you need. Try to understand, children. This is the safest place for you right now. We want you to be safe, so that we can all be together again after the war."

The visits always ended that way. I would walk back through the corridor, my face streaming with tears, convinced that Madame Kahn was lying to me. In my mind, no one was trustworthy; everyone lied. Emmy and Jean-Claude would hold my hands and whisper, "Just don't believe what the nuns say. They don't know." But it was easy for the Kahn children to be brave; they had seen their mother, talked to her, held her.

In the new year, I was promoted to a higher level. I was told that I had "caught up," and was now in the proper class. Sister Visitation was my teacher. The lessons were more difficult, but I was able to follow along. I knew that if I fell behind, I would be tapped with the ruler again in front of everyone.

The season of Lent came. The statues and the crucifix in the chapel were draped with purple cloths during that time. Even the priest wore purple vestments during mass. Purple was the color of penitence; we were to be reminded of Christ's Passion and death. When the nuns sang the Divine Office, as it was called, their chants sounded sad to me. I knew the Latin songs were about Christ's suffering on the cross. The Lenten season would last for forty days and forty nights. I remember how, on the first day, ashes were put on our foreheads in the shape of a cross. We had to "wear" the ashes all day long. It was Ash Wednesday. The priest said, "Remember that you are dust, and unto dust you shall return," as he marked our foreheads with the ashes. Some of the students made their first confessions during Lent. Sister Visitation told us that we were to remember that we were nothing more than dust, but through the Passion and death of Jesus, we could have eternal life.

We wore different colored smocks and our prayers seemed to take longer at vespers. I prayed always that God would let me go home to Maman and Papa. During Lent, we had to offer something up to the Lord, as a way of symbolically carrying the cross with Him. I did not know what to give up during Lent, so I gave up playing with Emmy during recreation. I also resolved never to speak of my parents again. It was the greatest sacrifice I could think of. Emmy and I sat on the cold stone benches and watched the other children laughing gaily in the courtyard. We were like two old women in a park, with nothing left to say.

Sundays came and went, but we did not get taken out of line for a visit with Madame Kahn anymore. Once in a while, I noticed that one of the other Jewish children was missing. We did not see Marguerite anymore, and Jean-Claude told us that one of the boys in his class had left the school. We were afraid to ask what had become of them.

One afternoon, in the spring, just before Easter, Sister Marie Louise took Emmy and me out of class. "I have been told to bring you to the dormitory," she said in a hushed tone.

When we got there, Sister Marie Louise told us to remove our smocks. She packed our clothes in our bags. We were allowed to keep the winter coats she had given us; we would need them. On the top of our bags, she placed our black prayer books and our rosaries from the bedside drawers. "Remember to say your prayers each night," she told us. "Pray for those who do not believe in God, and never forget your Holy Father in heaven." Emmy and I looked at each other but did not speak.

In the corridor, Jean-Claude was waiting for us. There was a satchel in his hand, his cap on his head. When I saw him standing there in his traveling clothes, I remember thinking that we were either going home or being taken away by the Nazis. The Nazis had come back for us.

"Hurry now, children," Sister Marie Louise told us.

She walked briskly ahead of us, down the stone steps and through the main corridor. We left the dormitory building and walked outside, following the stone path to the convent. The day was cloudy and windy; a light rain was falling. I felt I had been set free. For the first time that spring, I was aware of the scent of eucalyptus trees nearby, of the little buds on the branches of the cherry trees, and I wondered why we had not walked indoors to the convent. Sister led us up the stone steps into the darkened foyer. Mother Superior was there, waiting for us, her hands clasped inside her deep sleeves.

"Bring the children in to me," she told Sister Marie Louise, and then she disappeared into her office.

Sister Marie Louise smiled at us and hugged each one of us tightly. As she buttoned our coats, she said, "Today, you are going to leave us, children. It is a very sad day for us, but there is a family nearby that wishes to adopt you! Isn't that wonderful news? I hope you will be very happy in your new home. Perhaps you will come back to visit us from time to time."

I looked at Jean-Claude, my eyes wide, but he shook his head to let me know I should not protest.

Sister Marie Louise led us into the Mother Superior's office. She told us goodbye. As soon as the door had closed, the Mother Superior pointed to three straw-bottomed chairs that had been brought in for us. We were to sit and wait. I looked around, awed by the office. I had never seen such a room. There was a huge Oriental rug on the floor, a broad desk of dark wood, and a wide window behind the desk that looked out on the enclosed courtyard. I realized that Mother Superior had been able to see us, to watch us in the courtyard every day, during recreation. She must have seen a great deal during the past months.

"My children," she said to us, "we are expecting a car for you within the hour. If everything goes according to schedule, you will be leaving Sorèze this afternoon. I hope and pray for your safety during your journey, and I hope you will not forget all that you have learned here at the school. Your lessons are very important, and you must continue with them. I have asked Sister Marie Louise to pack the appropriate lesson books in your satchels."

None of us spoke. We were mesmerized by this woman and listened to her instructions as though she were preparing us for the rest of our lives. There were many books lying on her desk, and even more in the shelves to the rear of her office. I remember that one entire wall was lined with books. Mother Superior drew one book onto her lap, a large, heavy one, and told us that she would like to read to us until the car arrived. I could hear a clock ticking in the bookcase. Mother Superior found the place in the book, and she began to read. The passage was the Beatitudes, which we had learned in religion class, taken from the Gospel of Matthew:

Blessed are the poor in spirit:
for theirs is the kingdom of heaven.
Blessed are they that mourn:
for they shall be comforted.
Blessed are the meek:
for they shall possess the land.

Mother Superior turned a page and continued reading to us:

> And whosoever will force thee one mile, go with him another two. Give to him that asketh of thee, and from him that would borrow of thee, turn not away. You have heard that it hath been said, Thou shalt love thy neighbor and hate thy enemy. But I say to you, Love your enemies: do good to them that hate you: and pray for them that persecute and calumniate you. (Matthew 5)

Mother Superior closed the book and caressed the dark leather of its binding. She then stood up, went to the bookcase, and took out another large book and opened it to a place that was marked with a piece of paper. Standing in front of us, she smiled and said, "This prayer I am about to read to you is one of my favorite prayers. It is one with which your parents are probably familiar. It is often prayed in the synagogues. Not long ago, a rabbi came here to stay at Sorèze for several weeks, and he left this prayer book for us. He left only days before you children arrived. I will read this prayer to you:

> Master of the Universe! I herewith forgive anyone who may have irritated, angered, or injured me, whether acting against my person, my possessions, or my reputation. Let no man be punished on my account, whether the wrong done me was accidental or

malicious, unwitting or purposeful, by word or by deed. May it be Your will, O Lord my God and God of my fathers, that I sin no more. May I never again anger You by doing that which is evil in Your sight. I pray that You will wipe away my sins, not through sickness and suffering, but with great mercy. May the words of my mouth and the meditation of my heart be acceptable before You, O Lord, my Rock and my Redeemer.

There was silence when she had stopped reading, and the Mother Superior closed the book, placed it on her desk, and went to stand by the window. She rested her hands on the wooden sill and stood with her back to us, waiting. As the old clock on the bookcase ticked on, we barely moved in our seats. It was hot in the office, and I wanted to take off my coat. I remember watching the nun and wondering who she was. Why was she so mysterious? Had she no other name, no other life, besides "Mother Superior"?

There was the faintest sound of a bell far in the distance.

Mother Superior turned to us, smiling. "It is time, children. I will walk with you as far as the gate."

We stood up and took hold of our satchels. Mother Superior followed us out into the foyer and then into the cold. We walked in the rain across the courtyard toward the wooden gate, where the gatekeeper stood, waiting to let us out. Even in the wind, Mother Superior did not hurry; she did not allow herself to shiver from the cold. I watched her walking slowly, her hands clasped inside her sleeves. She glided through the courtyard, while Emmy and Jean-Claude raced ahead. I had never wanted to run so much in my life, but I continued walking, following closely behind the Mother Superior.

Just before we reached the gatekeeper, Mother Superior stopped and faced the three of us. One small hand emerged from her sleeve. She extended it for each of us to shake. "*Au revoir*, children. God go with you."

"Thank you, Mother," we said.

Her hand went back into her wide sleeves, and she held the sleeves together so neither hand could be seen anymore. She turned and walked back to the convent, slowly again, despite the driving rain. I watched her veil blowing in the wind as it had on the first day. I would never see her again.

The gatekeeper, a short, gnarled old man, said, "Patience, children," as he unbolted the door. Then he opened it and we were standing in the street. The wooden door to the convent of Sorèze bolted behind us. We looked up and down the street, and then we saw the black car at the bottom of the hill. Madame Kahn was waving to us. She was standing by the car door, waiting.

We all started to run at the same time. None of us shouted or laughed or screamed. We ran in silence, as fast as we could, carrying that mysterious silence of Sorèze within us.

When we reached the car, Emmy and Jean-Claude cried, "Maman!" She hugged us all and hurried us into the backseat of the car. As soon as she started the engine and we had turned around, heading back up the street, I knew we were going home. As we passed the stone walls of the school for the last time, I did not want to look at it, and I turned away. I had never seen a prison, but in my mind, it was as if I had just escaped from one.

It took me months to forget the sickening sensation in my stomach with which I had awakened every morning at Sorèze. As many times as I had imagined that Maman and Papa must be alive, I had just as often persuaded myself that they were dead. Why else had they abandoned me, split up our family, and left me in the hands of strangers, if they had not believed that they were truly going to die that year of 1943?

PART THREE: LIBERATION

August 1944 to June 1946

. . . out of sorrow into happiness, out of mourning into a holiday, out of darkness into daylight, and out of bondage into redemption.

—Passover Haggadah

Reunion at Arthès

Madame Kahn stops the car in front of her apartment in St. Juéry, and we all get out quickly. There is no sign of Maman or Papa, no sign of anyone. Then a man slips out from behind the garden gate; he has been hiding, waiting for us. Without a word, Madame Kahn turns the car over to him. He gets into it and drives away.

"Slowly, slowly," Madame Kahn says as we rush up the walk to her apartment. It comes back to me suddenly, the feeling that we are being watched. I have been at Sorèze for five months and have forgotten about constantly having to look over my shoulder. I see that some of the flowers are starting to come up in the garden. The last time I was here, I saw only the dried grass and leaves. Jean-Claude starts to run. In a moment, he is gone behind the house, opening the door, and going in the back way. We follow him. We enter the house, and there, in the kitchen, are Monsieur Kahn, Aunt Hanna, and Andrée Fedou. I run to Aunt Hanna and she holds me in her arms.

"Oh, Renée," she says, "you mustn't worry. Your parents are alive and safe. They are waiting for you. We know how terrified you have been, but your Maman could not come. It would have been too dangerous, for you and for her. Your Maman did not want to put you in the convent, but it was for your own protection. Madame Kahn and I persuaded her to do it. The police arrests were getting worse, and children were being taken away every week. We had to think of some way to protect you, and we heard that Catholic schools and convents were taking in Jewish children—"

"I just want to see Maman!" I say, unable to contain my tears any longer. Andrée stands up and holds out her hand. I am to go with her. I do not even remember to say goodbye to Emmy and Jean-Claude. I only want to see my parents. I do not want to wait any longer.

I hug Aunt Hanna once more, and then Madame Kahn, for bringing me back to the village. Then I look back to wave at Emmy. She never lets go of her mother's hand.

I follow Andrée out the door and into the street. She looks different—thinner. She is chatting all the way, telling me how many times the police have come to search their apartment, how many times her father has had to hide in the fields. I want to say, "You think that's bad?" but I keep silent. Nothing can bring me to talk about Sorèze, now that I am back in the village.

We must walk all the way from St. Juéry to Arthès. As soon as we have crossed the bridge over the river Tarn, I see the *tabac* sign on the front of our building. If the metal shutters were open, I know Papa and Maman would be at the windows, waiting for me, but there is no sign of life. From the outside, the building looks deserted.

Andrée leads me down another street. We do not go to my parents' apartment, nor to the Fedous'. I know we are following the route to my old school, but before we get there, we turn right, down another deserted street. My satchel is heavy in my hand. We follow the street halfway down until we reach an alley on the left. "Down here," says Andrée. We walk along the dark alley where the gutter runs down the middle. There is a stairway on the right. "Come this way," Andrée tells me. She leads me up the stairs. We walk up two flights and then stop before a dark door. Andrée uses a secret knock. In a moment, her mother opens the door.

I slip inside. Maman and Papa are the first ones I see, and I run to them. I feel I am in a dream. I can hardly believe they are alive and standing in front of me. They are all laughing with joy at the way I cling to Maman, crying. Maman is crying, too. We cannot say anything. I go to Papa, and he hugs me, too.

"Don't cry now, Renée, you're back home!" he says. Then he turns to the others. "She's grown," he observes.

"Yes," Maman agrees. "She's growing up."

Maman wipes my face with a handkerchief and looks at my gloves and coat. Hardly able to speak, she asks, "Who gave you these?"

"Sister Marie Louise."

"That was kind of her. They make you look like a young lady, Renée."

I do not talk about the convent, the Mother Superior, about the candies that were taken away. "Why didn't you come to see me, Maman?"

"It was not possible," she says, hugging me. "We would have been spotted by the police and taken away. They know about us. Only Madame Kahn could go, since she is French. We had to pretend that you were French so they would allow you to stay at the convent."

"Why are we here?" I ask, looking around at the grim interior of the apartment. The walls are covered with rotting wallpaper, the floorboards are warped. It is quite a contrast to the pristine rooms at Sorèze. "Why can't we go to our own apartment?"

Maman says that Monsieur Fedou told her to stay out of the apartment for a while. He found this room for us to stay in until things quiet down in the village.

Monsieur Fedou has set up the radio so that we will be able to listen to the BBC tonight. I am surprised to see that he still allows the radio. We had heard in the convent of how dangerous it is to have a radio; anyone caught listening to the BBC would be arrested by the police on sight.

It is late afternoon. Madame Fedou and Maman have prepared food for us. There is very little to eat; only some stale bread, tomatoes that are not yet ripe, a few boiled eggs. Once more, I will have to get used to having very little food to eat, and to rooms that have no heat. We keep our coats on. I sit next to Papa, and he tells me stories about the farm where he was hidden in the Black Mountain region. It's as if Papa wants to keep me from talking: if I begin to talk about being separated from Maman and from him, he knows I will begin to cry again.

Papa had lived in a hamlet, north of Carcassone, where there were four farms. A peasant farmer for whom Papa had worked had sheltered him until the end of December, not knowing that Papa was Jewish.

Papa slept in the grain storeroom at the farm. Each night, rats would come out and crawl over Papa, trying to get to the grain. One morning, Papa finally protested to the farmer. "I would rather be with the cows than with the rats!" he said. "If you don't move the grain, I'm leaving you!"

"*Non! Non!*" the peasant had cried. "I will move the grain."

After that, there was nothing the farmer would not do for Papa. He needed Papa's help on the farm, since so many men in the area had either been killed in the early months of the war or had joined the Resistance groups and had gone into hiding.

Papa had liked the farmhouse and described it to me. It

had stone floors, low-beamed ceilings, an open fireplace with a simple carved mantel above it, and straw-bottomed chairs to sit on. Papa and the farmer would sit up late at night exchanging stories of the war, but Papa never admitted to the farmer that he was Jewish. Often, they would wake up before dawn, angry with themselves that they had so many chores to attend to and had spent so much time talking the night before.

"How did you get home, Papa?" I asked.

"The Protestant minister came back for me. He had heard a report that an ordinance had been passed whereby all the men who had served in the war, including members of the Foreign Legion, were immune from future roundups or arrest. He said I couldn't be arrested. He told me it was my duty to go home and look after Maman. He had heard from the Fedous that Maman was afraid to stay alone in the apartment and had been living at the Valats'. So I came back with the minister. But in spite of what he told me, we continued to hide in the fields whenever we heard about roundups in the area."

"I have been afraid that the Germans are using this ordinance as a ploy to bring all the Jews out of hiding," Maman murmured.

"Yes," Papa agreed. "We cannot be sure the police will abide by the ordinance. When it comes down to it, not a single Jew is immune."

Papa had left the farm at the end of December, "just after the holiday," he said. For Christmas, the old farmer had killed a pig. He had butchered and bled it, then fried the blood the way many peasants do when they harvest the grapes.

I wrinkled up my nose in disgust.

"I told him," Papa continued, "I don't like this, old man. I don't like red meat!"

The farmer had looked at Papa as though he were crazy. "Are you kidding, Monsieur? This is the best part! If I didn't know better, I would think you are Jewish!"

Papa had laughed aloud, and the peasant with him. When

Papa left the farm, the peasant wept and gave Papa a nine-pound duck.

We all laughed at Papa's stories. Monsieur Fedou adjusted the radio, and we settled into chairs to listen to the broadcast. But I did not listen. I looked at Maman's and Papa's faces and wondered whether I was truly safe. Maman had told me we would never be separated again. I wondered how I would ever tell her all that had happened to me, all the nightmarish thoughts that had crossed my mind while I had been at the convent. For five months, it was as if I had lived another life. I knew Maman would never understand.

After the broadcast was over, the Fedous stood up to leave. We said goodbye to them, and Madame Fedou kissed my cheeks and said, "Welcome back, Renée!" Andrée gave me a hug. Then they went down the narrow stairs and quickly walked back through the alley, the same way Andrée and I had come.

It was quiet in the room after the Fedous had left, and I did not know what to say to Maman and Papa. They prepared a place for me to sleep on an old mattress in the corner of the room. I began to unpack my satchel. Maman looked over my clothes and was upset by the fact that so many of my dresses were too short, or had frayed collars or tears in the material. "Didn't they mend your clothes, Renée?" she asked. This was the only question she ever asked me about my stay at Sorèze. It was too difficult for her to talk about the time we had been separated.

Maman and Papa began to clean the apartment. I found my rosary and knelt down beside the mattress on which I was to sleep that night. I blessed myself with the crucifix, and I began to pray the rosary. I wanted to thank Christ for bringing me home to my family. I heard Papa say behind me, "Lissy, what is she doing?"

Maman answered, "Let her alone. It's much safer this way. People will believe we're Catholics, not Jews. Let her say the prayers."

I knew that I must not forget my Holy Father in heaven, as

Sister Marie Louise had told us when we left Sorèze, yet I felt strange praying the rosary in front of my parents. There was no crucifix on the wall, no figure of Christ or of Our Lady to look at as I prayed, yet I prayed anyway. I prayed for those who did not believe in God. I prayed for the Jewish children who were left at Sorèze, that they would soon be with their parents. My own parents looked away. They did not understand, and I did not know how to explain it to them.

In the spring, we were always at the Valats' house, listening to the radio. The BBC reports were often confusing and contradictory. When would the Allies land on French soil?

I did not want to return to school, and Maman let me stay home. She said she did not want us to be separated any longer. I continued with my lessons in the workbook that Sister Marie Louise had given me. By the end of May, I had completed the lessons, and Maman said I was too advanced for the *école communale*. Papa did not work for the factory anymore; the supervisor had warned him that inspections were still going on. He told Papa to stay out of the way, regardless of whether or not he was immune.

I don't remember leaving the apartment, except to get water at the pump for Maman or to go to the Valats'. Monsieur Valat and Monsieur Fedou would go to the café, and they would bring us news of the village. The town crier had not discovered our whereabouts and he never bothered us again.

During the first week of June, the radio BBC broadcast was always the same. For days, they gave the first line of a poem by Paul Verlaine:

Les sanglots longs
Des violons
De l'automne
[The long sobs of autumn violins . . .]

Monsieur Fedou said that it was a signal to put all of France on the alert. He told us that everyone throughout the entire two villages was in a state of suspense. What was worse, that first week of June was unusually hot in the South. We sweltered in the hidden apartment where the windows could hardly be cracked for air. There was scarcely any breeze until nightfall. We were all on edge, wondering what would happen next.

At last, one night, the weather broke with a thunderstorm. The storm was at its greatest intensity during the BBC broadcast, and we sat in the tiny apartment with the Fedous and the Valats, who had come just minutes before the storm began. We hardly moved, since we were straining so hard to hear the report. Through the static, a man's voice said something about singing, but no one heard what he said except Papa. "The phrase sounded like, '*Le coq chantera ce soir* [The rooster will sing tonight],'" he told us. Soon after, the second line of Verlaine's poem was finally given:

Bercent mon cœur
D'une langueur
Monotone.
[. . . Soothe my heart with dull languor.]

The moment he heard these words, Monsieur Fedou's face broke into a grin. He stood up to turn off the radio and left the apartment immediately. Monsieur Valat and Papa debated over the meaning of the broadcast. Monsieur Valat said that since the symbol for France was the rooster, the clue given must mean that France would soon be liberated. Papa's eyes were filled with hope and expectation.

The next morning, June sixth, I awoke to the sounds of shouting and singing below our apartment. Church bells were ringing, and people everywhere below us were laughing uncontrollably. Papa opened the shutters and saw men and women below, gathered in the street, shouting and dancing. Others were hurrying toward the *tabac* to hear the news. Windows opened, and other people, still half asleep, asked what was happening.

We dressed hurriedly, then ran down into the street. The Allies had landed in Normandy! It was the beginning of our liberation, D day, the sixth of June. Papa and Maman embraced; both of them had faces wet with tears. We all laughed at the same time, and Maman and Papa kissed me over and over. An accordionist appeared out of nowhere and began to play. The Valats and Fedous were dancing in the street. I felt that all the days and nights of living clandestinely had been erased by that one morning of joy.

Our happiness following D day was marred by the debilitating effects of four years of occupation. It was almost impossible, by that time, to get food. Maman had already sold every piece of linen, silver, and jewelry she had been able to take with her into hiding. In summer, we had vegetables, but there was no way to store anything. Papa's face was always drawn and serious, and I knew he was thinking about Aunt Sophie and Jeannette.

After D day, Arthès and St. Juéry imposed curfews. There were many bombardments by the Allies, and the German troops were retreating. Papa was not sure we would be able to stay in the village. When there were alerts or air raids, we were forced to leave the village and take cover in the fields. Papa thought the Sauts du Tarn factory might be a target for bomber planes flying overhead. We would stay in the fields for hours, until all was silent in the village, and it was then that I came to realize what Maman's and Papa's lives had been like while I had been safely hidden in the convent. I would often lie there in the field, as we waited for silence, thinking about the Mother Superior, Sister Marie Louise, and Sister Présentation. I wondered about the other Jewish children hidden there, especially Véronique. Would she survive?

The wait for freedom, and liberation, became agonizing. Uncle Oscar and Aunt Hanna returned from Albi to the village. Raymonde and Evelyne were with them. Only with them, and with Emmy and Jean-Claude, could I exchange stories about being in the convent. They understood how mysterious, sometimes peaceful, and oftentimes bewildering a place it had been. The grownups listened to the BBC as often as possible. Papa believed it would all be over by the end of the summer.

Many strangers passed through the village, some staying with us. I remember one morning a Russian soldier coming in off the street, hoping for a meal and a place to stay. The Fedous took him in because they had the room, but Maman and Papa were often called in to talk with him, since the soldier could speak some German but no French. He loved to play cards and taught me many card games and tricks. When he left, he gave me a deck of cards.

When the Royal Air Force bombed the last German airfields, Albi was set afire. We heard the bombardments, and I remember everyone running into the street, shouting, *"Les Anglais! Les Anglais bombardent!"* Papa and I climbed a steep hill beyond my school, from which we could see Albi in the distance, since it was only two and a half miles (four kilometers) from Arthès. We saw Albi ablaze. As we stood there, high above the village, Papa and I smiled, tasting true freedom for the first time in years. We looked out over all the tiled rooftops of Arthès and St. Juéry, the river Tarn, and, in the distance, the city of Albi. At last, our period of hiding was over. We later learned that the post office in Albi had been bombed. I wondered about the postal clerk who had offered Madame Kahn the use of his car to take us to Sorèze, but we never discovered what became of him.

What had once been the Southern Zone was liberated when the Allies landed in the Fréjus area on August 15, 1944. One week later, Toulon was liberated. Everyone in Arthès rushed into the streets, shrieking once more; it was a repeat of D day. We saw the Fedous, the Valats, and others acting crazy with relief and joy. People were rushing from door to door, knocking and calling their neighbors and friends. French flags appeared in the windows and were draped from balconies. Everyone was shouting, "Liberation! France is free!" We caught sight of Uncle Oscar and Aunt Hanna, Raymonde and Evelyne. The church bells were ringing and did not stop until nightfall. Maman and Aunt Hanna hugged each other and cried. We had survived.

We lived much more openly after that. There were reports from Albi of spontaneous acts of violence against those who had collaborated with the enemy. The town crier was shot by a member of the Resistance on the day after liberation. Known denouncers were brought out of hiding in Albi and had their heads shaved; others were shot and killed on the spot.

One night, perhaps the night of the liberation, I remember going to kneel by my bed. We were back in our old apartment, above the *tabac*. I began to pray the rosary. I wanted to give thanks to God for giving us freedom. I prayed the Our Father and the Hail Mary. Then Maman came up beside me and said, "Renée, the war is over. You don't have to do that anymore."

Papa told me that we were safe now, but I wasn't even sure what that meant, or how to behave. I could not remember a time in my life when we were not hiding.

Paris

Papa returned to work at the Sauts du Tarn, continuing until October of 1945.

Our last year in Arthès was, in some ways, more difficult than all the others had been. We truly learned the meaning of the word deprivation. There was no heat in winter, and our food supplies were meager. In the winter, Maman knitted constantly to provide warm sweaters for us. We slept bundled in blankets and fully clothed. We lived on eggs, potatoes, cheese, and bread.

When the Germans finally surrendered to the Allies on May 7, 1945, we could at last believe in our freedom. But the retreat of the Nazi forces had left France in ruins. The Nazis had burned buildings, sabotaged railway tracks, destroyed entire towns, and shot people dead in the streets. We heard about the horrible massacre at Oradour-sur-Glane, a village located outside of Limoges. Limoges, for the most part, had been sympathetic to the plight of Jewish refugees during the war. Forced to retreat, the Nazis initiated a mad rampage of revenge. They had entered the village, shot all the local men who still remained by the end of the war, and then had taken nearly five hundred women and children to the Catholic church with the local priest. The villagers were locked in the church, with their pastor, and burned alive. The Nazis then set fire to the entire village, leaving it in smoldering ruins. Theirs was a bitter and vengeful withdrawal from France.

In our small village, it took us months to shake the sensation of constantly being watched. We were little by little confronted with stories on the radio and in the newspapers about what the Nazis had done to the Jews in their factories of horror, the death camps. Maman and Papa tried to keep the knowledge of the atrocities from me as long as possible, but they were finally no longer able to disguise their anger and disgust. Papa became silent and withdrawn; he thought constantly of our family in Germany.

Papa had the idea that there were no Jews left. We had survived, he thought, simply because we had been fortunate enough to find the small village of Arthès when we did. Other Jews who had come to the village in the height of the occupation had been taken away long before they had had a chance to establish contacts, or even to find a decent room. We never forgot how indebted we were to the Fedous and the Valats for their vigilance in protecting us.

Uncle Oscar and his family were the first to return to Paris. Uncle Oscar was not certain whether he could reclaim "La Standard," the family clothing business. He told Papa, "You stay here until I find something for us in Paris." They left St. Juéry days later. Our farewell was brief and emotional. Maman and Aunt Hanna could only cling to each other and say, "We've been through so much together. Let's hope that we will know happiness from now on." Aunt Hanna was still afraid that some disaster would befall them on their way to Paris.

"We will follow you to Paris soon," Papa said.

After Uncle Oscar, Aunt Hanna, and my cousins left, Papa

was silent and brooded for hours. He wrote several letters to Aunt Sophie in Toulouse but received no response. All he could think of was having the family reunited. I noticed he never spoke of Uncle Heinrich.

A letter soon came from Uncle Oscar, describing the family's journey to Paris. They had gone as far as Orléans, but part of the train tracks had been bombed, so they were forced to walk a long distance around and pick up another train for Paris on the other side. When Uncle Oscar arrived and went to their old apartment, the proprietor refused to rent it back to him. "La Standard" had been sold by the Germans to a Frenchman, and Uncle Oscar would have to go through legal proceedings to reclaim his business. He told Papa in his letter that it was still too early for us to return to Paris, as everything was in a state of chaos. "Stay in Arthès," Aunt Hanna had added at the bottom of the letter, "where things are saner."

As 1945 came to an end, Maman and Papa spoke more and more of returning to Paris. Papa was anxious to establish contact with the Red Cross and await the returning trains. He was convinced that if the members of our family in Germany had survived, they would ask to be brought to Paris, since the last communication they had had from Maman and Papa would have been letters written in September of 1939, informing their families of their whereabouts. Foremost in Papa's mind were Aunt Sophie and Jeannette. Papa was determined to find them first, in Toulouse, and then make our way back to Paris.

By February of 1946, my parents were ready to leave Arthès. Our bundles were pitifully small; after five years of living in hiding, we had almost nothing left. The Fedous, the Valats, the Kahns, the Protestant minister, and even the supervisor from the Sauts du Tarn factory came to say goodbye to us. It was when I tried to say goodbye to Emmy and Jean-Claude that I began to cry uncontrollably; we would always have between us a special bond, though we rarely spoke about our stay at Sorèze. There were tears and awkward silences as Maman and Papa tried to express their gratitude to the people of the village. Madame Valat hugged me on our way out the door; she told me she would never forget the day I had wandered over to her house.

As the rickety bus pulled away from the curb, we waved to our friends. I remember staring out the window, a lump in my throat, as I tried to hold back tears of regret; part of me was afraid to leave the village, for fear of what we were going to find in Toulouse and Paris. And, once again, I was leaving friends who truly loved me and had taken care of me. As we boarded the train in Albi and found places by the window, Papa took our hands, Maman's and mine, and held them tight, as if to say, "From now on, whatever we are to go through, we go through it together."

The train was filled with people; many of them were refugees who were on their way to Toulouse or to Paris. Most of the people were traveling alone; we were one of the few families on the train, and I remember how the passengers stared at us with bewildered looks. So rare was it, in those days, to see that some people had somehow managed to end up together.

Our first stop was Toulouse. Through the Red Cross center, the Protestant minister had been able to locate Uncle Heinrich's family, and had written an address for Papa on a slip of paper the day before we left Arthès. When we arrived in Toulouse, we walked for several blocks until we reached the correct address. It was the home of another Jewish family, that of Jeannette's best friend.

Our reunion with my cousin left us tearful and shaken. The father of Jeannette's friend took us into a sparsely furnished room and allowed us to speak with Jeannette alone for several hours. I remember how silent those first few minutes were; all of us found it difficult to talk. Jeannette had grown thin, and there were dark circles under her eyes. She told Maman and Papa that Aunt Sophie had been arrested.

"*Oh, non!*" cried Maman.

"Just before the South was liberated," Jeannette told us in a weak voice. "I went out with Maman for food. We hardly had anything left, and we were just trying to buy something to eat. We knew we could only shop from three o'clock to four o'clock in the afternoon, and that we could not enter any department or retail stores. But the Germans were spot-checking that day in the street, and two soldiers stopped Maman. They asked to see her identity card and accused her of having gone into a department store, which we had not done. Also, it was three minutes after four.

"When they looked over Maman's card," Jeannette continued, "and then looked at mine, they said, 'These are false,' and arrested Maman right there in the street."

I felt tears come to my eyes and I ran to Jeannette. I was crying for her, remembering how I had felt without Maman at Sorèze, but I did not know how to comfort her.

"They told me to go home," Jeanette went on, "and wait for Maman. They said she would be back home the next day, but she never came back. Every day, for weeks, I went to the Red Cross center for information, but they never had any news.

"At least, not until last week," Jeannette added haltingly. "They contacted me and said they had information about Maman. When I went down to the center, they told me Maman had been sent first to Caserne de Caffareli, where she had lived in the barracks, and then she had been deported to Auschwitz, where she had survived until the liberation. But on the train—" Jeannette sobbed and couldn't go on.

"On the train," she said after a moment, "she died of typhus. She died on the train that was bringing her back to me!"

That was when we all broke down. I remember there was

a clock on a bookshelf in that room, like the one on the Mother Superior's bookcase in the office at Sorèze, and there were just the sounds of the clock ticking and of us sobbing. Maman held Jeannette in her arms and tried to comfort her. Papa tried to persuade her to come with us to Paris, but Jeannette was determined to stay in Toulouse with her friends.

After a while, we had to leave for the station. Papa thanked the man who had taken care of Jeannette and promised to stay in touch with her. As soon as he was able, he would begin to send money for her. I clung to Jeannette as we said goodbye; I was thinking of how happy she had been in Toulouse, with so many friends, in 1942. Now, four years later, she was totally changed: broken, frightened, and helpless.

The train pulls into the Gare d'Austerlitz in the early morning. For me, it is the first time I have come to Paris, for I don't remember the Paris of 1939. The city is cold and gray. How dark Paris is, I think, so dark, compared to the warm South, to Arthès. Maman and Papa hardly speak as we linger at the station, adjusting to our surroundings. I can see how apprehensive my parents are. But Papa knows where to go. All around us, there are people who look very thin. Maman says they are poverty-stricken souls who have weathered four years of occupation by the Nazis in Paris. Papa has a slip of paper with an address. We are to go there, but we must walk. There are no cabs, no buses. We walk a long time. We are used to it.

The building is 176 Rue du Temple. This is where we will live. We walk under a brown arch and, to our left, there is a door leading into the building. Maman takes me up the curving stairs to the first floor. There is a window that looks out onto the rear courtyard. We are to live on the first floor.

Inside our apartment, there are a table and three chairs. There are two old beds. Three plates are in the cupboard, three cups, three spoons, forks, and knives. These have been provided for us by the O.S.E. (Oeuvre de Secours aux Enfants). I am to go to the O.S.E., to the dispensary, for shots and medical attention, because I have been in hiding. I dread the shots, but Papa says I am weak and need them, and the people will be good to me.

Later, Maman and I walk past buildings that have been partially demolished, streets that are closed off. We have ration cards. Mine says "J-3" because I am over six years old. In the stores, you can finally buy shirts, pajamas, underwear, but it costs Maman one of her textile cards. Only one article per customer is allowed, and the shoppers become angry.

We learn that people all around us had denounced Jews to the Gestapo. Someone in the courtyard tells Maman not to buy from the corner baker nor from the dairy man on our street. "They denounced Jews throughout the war," we are told.

I go to the elementary school, and they call me *sale juif* in the playground after school. It means "dirty Jew." Now I know what anti-Semitism is. A classmate takes my snack away from me, and the teacher ignores it. I run home, in tears, to Maman. She is furious. There are so few Jewish children for me to befriend. What she wants most is for me to learn about my religion and not to be afraid of it any longer. I join Les Petites Ailes (The Little Wings). It is a Jewish scout organization. We have outings on the weekends and will go camping in the summers. Raymonde has joined, too. Our leader is five or six years older than we are and is called "Caiman," or Crocodile. All the leaders have the names of animals. Years from now, Raymonde will meet Caiman again at a country club, only to learn that Caiman also is named Ruth, and that she and her mother had survived the Warsaw ghetto in Poland.

I have only Jewish friends. I am still waiting to hear about Uncle Heinrich. No one ever talks about him. I think Papa knows what happened to him but will not tell us.

Soon, the Red Cross contacts Maman. It is the end of 1946.

They have identified Maman's father and her stepmother, who have been in the concentration camp called Theresienstadt. They are alive and they are coming to live with us. Maman tries to prepare a place for them in our small apartment. She is worried there will not be enough food for them. She talks to me openly one night about how my grandparents will look. "I don't want to frighten you, Renée, but try not to be too upset by their appearance. They have been through a horrible time and have had hardly anything to eat. We cannot imagine how bad it was for them—"

My grandparents are not coming for several days. I try not to think about it. I go to school and play with my friends at our scout meetings. Maman takes me shopping along the Rue des Rosiers, where one can buy kosher food.

One afternoon, when I come home from school, Maman and Papa are not there. They have left the door open for me, and candy is on the table. I go outside, down to the courtyard, to jump rope. Everything echoes because of the cement and the high walls of the surrounding buildings. I am there, by myself, when they arrive. I see them coming slowly under the arch. Papa holds my grandfather by the arm, and my grandmother is supported by Maman. They look very old, and there are dark, reddish circles under their eyes. They are the thinnest people I have ever seen. Maman calls to me.

I drop the rope and walk to them. "This is Ruth," says Maman, and my grandfather smiles. I don't know what to do, so I hug them both. They hold on to me as if it has been years since anyone has touched them with kindness.

Maman takes care of my grandparents. She gives them some of her food, but they don't know it is hers. They never speak about the concentration camp when I'm around. When I ask Maman why, she says, "Everyone is so broken down, Ruth." She has slipped back to calling me Ruth.

Uncle Oscar and Aunt Hanna are nearby. We go to visit them often. Uncle Oscar finally returns to his rainwear manufacturing plant, and Papa is able to join him in a parallel branch. Each morning, they assemble the raincoats down in the courtyard. There are always racks and racks of coats.

I am now eight years old. In the afternoons I go to my scout meetings. I tell all my friends about my grandparents and what happened to them. Everyone looks sad for us. I keep thinking Uncle Heinrich will come soon and then I won't feel lonely anymore. He will read to me again and play in the courtyard with me. I will tell all my friends about how my Uncle Heinrich has returned from the camps.

School is at the *école primaire*, but I don't like to go there. When the teachers return my papers, there are no comments or grades on them. It's as if I am not really in school, as if I do not exist. But the other students—who do not have names like Cohen or Levi—their papers have comments written all over them, especially if the paper belongs to someone with a noble name, with a "de" in it.

When the mail comes for Maman and Papa, they always stand right at the door, looking through the envelopes. One afternoon, there are envelopes for both of them. They are messages from the Red Cross. Maman and Papa sit down on the chairs and slowly open the envelopes. It takes a long time for Papa to read the contents. There are several forms. Maman covers her face with her hand.

Then my father breaks down, too.

He makes no effort to stop the tears rolling down his face. He sobs aloud. In his hands is the proof of what became of his family. Uncle Heinrich had been interned at the Camp du Vernet before being deported. He, as well as Sittie, Hettie, and my father's mother, were gassed at Auschwitz. They have been dead for four years. Maman's sister, Lottie, also perished. They are never coming back.

There is a heavy silence in our apartment that night. We

say prayers for the members of our family who have died such abominable deaths. Papa does not talk. In my bed that night, I cry for my favorite uncle whom I can never talk to again. Each time I close my eyes, I have a horrible vision of Uncle Heinrich crammed into something called a gas chamber. Maman comes in to me. "What about Jeannette?" I ask her. Now she has no one.

Maman only shakes her head. "We will help her somehow," she says.

Sometime after we receive the records on Uncle Heinrich, I am in the Parc Louis XIII, sitting on a bench, doing homework, waiting for my scout meeting to begin. I watch two little girls playing catch at the other end of the park. Their faces are happy, completely absorbed in the game. They sing a song as they throw the ball back and forth. When I stand up and walk toward the gate to leave the park, I notice a book lying facedown on the grass. Its binding is red, and the cover looks vaguely familiar to me. I think one of the girls has dropped it from her satchel, so I pick it up to return it. When I open it to the first page, I see the familiar illustrations, the words that I had memorized long ago. It is a copy of *Le Petit Chaperon Rouge,* the story Uncle Heinrich had read to me almost every afternoon in Toulouse. I know the story by heart, and yet I read it again, tears swimming in my eyes, as I sit in the park, trying to find my way back to Toulouse, to that time before all the bad things happened to us.

Just for a moment, I am there, sitting on Uncle Heinrich's lap, laughing.

Afterword
by Ruth Kapp Hartz

It wasn't until the end of the war that I realized what much of the French population had done during the occupation. Because of our experience in the south of France, I had believed that ninety percent of the French people had been involved in Resistance activity. How wrong I had been.

Despite the fear with which we had lived in all the years of hiding from the French police and the Nazis during the war, it was not until I returned with my parents to Paris that I experienced open anti-Semitism. So many French people had collaborated with the Nazis that eighty thousand Jews had been deported by the time France was liberated.

Paris, in 1946, was still in shock; no one knew how to behave, how to resume normal living. Many people continued to perpetuate the inhumane treatment they had exhibited during the occupation. They would refuse to turn over apartments, businesses, or possessions that had once belonged to Jews who now came to reclaim what was rightfully theirs.

Small merchants blamed the Jews for their economic difficulties; the black market merchants resented the Jews because their own corrupt practices had been brought to an end with the liberation of France, and they could no longer take advantage of people.

How can one account for the different treatment we received from the people of southern France? Why were so many of them willing to endanger their own lives to work for the Resistance and shelter Jewish families? Many of the Jews who survived the occupation of France owe their lives to these stalwart country folk who literally did not know the meaning of the words "Jews" and "anti-Semitism." *"Qu'est-ce que c'est au juste un juif?"* they often asked Papa. "What is a Jew, really?"

In the late 1960s, my husband, Harry, accompanied me to the south of France. I inquired about the Fedou and Valat families at the Bureau du Tarn, and we made our way first to the village of Arthès. The village had not changed much in the intervening years, although the proportions seemed different to me. Houses that had once seemed so high were actually not so at all. The latrines where my father had hidden were apartments. We located the apartment where I had hidden with my parents, and there discovered Andrée Fedou, now living upstairs with her own family. There were tears in our eyes as she recognized me, and I her. Words were not necessary; an amazing bond already existed between us. I met Andrée's fifteen-year-old daughter and introduced my husband.

Lucette Fedou was in St. Juéry. She gathered all the Fedous together under one roof and held a special celebration for us. Lucette, we learned, was a grandmother, and Madame Fedou, a great-grandmother. The celebration was more of a reunion between long-lost friends than a reliving of past events. We did not discuss the war years, only what had happened since. The Fedous were so happy for me, and so excited to meet my American husband!

It never occurred to the Fedous to explain their actions, why they had risked their lives to save my family. For them, it was the natural thing to do. To this day, they probably are unable to fathom why so many had remained indifferent at best—at worst, had actually collaborated with the Nazis.

Many memories of the war rushed back to me as I visited with the Fedous. For me, the circle was complete, and there was some closure in that return to the villages. I saw how authentic and sincere these people were, and I experienced a sense of peace and gratitude that had long eluded me.

Their acts of bravery, committed on a daily basis, arose out of the dictates of the collective conscience of the village people. It was not necessarily thought out or even discussed. There was a need, and they rose to the occasion. The people of Arthès, whether Gaullist, Christian, Communist, or Socialist, came from a common heritage of persecution. Their ancestors had suffered the injustices of the feudal system, and even of the Church itself, as well as those of the more recent nineteenth and twentieth centuries. Perhaps this gave them a sixth sense of unknown mission, deep within, when confronted with the evil of the Holocaust. The immediate suffering experienced by the Jews in their midst was a reality they reacted to almost instinctively. Many of these righteous Gentiles died because of the humanitarian acts they performed.

In addition to being a personal chronicle, this book is a testimony to their natural heroism. Their actions, on behalf of so many innocents, have left us a legacy that must be remembered, and which, if fulfilled, will help to prevent a recurrence of such horrors in future years.